Sun Certified Enterprise Architect for Java™ EE Study Guide

Second Edition

Sun Certified Enterprise Architect for Java™ EE Study Guide

Second Edition

Mark Cade and Humphrey Sheil

PRENTICE HALL

Upper Saddle River, NJ • Boston • Indianapolis • San Francisco
New York • Toronto • Montreal • London • Munich • Paris • Madrid
Cape Town • Sydney • Tokyo • Singapore • Mexico City

Many of the designations used by manufacturers and sellers to distinguish their products are claimed as trademarks. Where those designations appear in this book, and the publisher was aware of a trademark claim, the designations have been printed with initial capital letters or in all capitals.

Sun Microsystems, Inc. has intellectual property rights relating to implementations of the technology described in this publication. In particular, and without limitation, these intellectual property rights may include one or more U.S. patents, foreign patents, or pending applications.

Sun, Sun Microsystems, the Sun logo, J2ME, J2EE, Java Card, and all Sun and Java based trademarks and logos are trademarks or registered trademarks of Sun Microsystems, Inc., in the United States and other countries. UNIX is a registered trademark in the United States and other countries, exclusively licensed through X/Open Company, Ltd. This publication is provided "as is" without warranty of any kind, either express or implied, including, but not limited to, the implied warranties of merchantability, fitness for a particular purpose, or non-infringement. This publication could include technical inaccuracies or typographical errors. Changes are periodically added to the information herein; these changes will be incorporated in new editions of the publication. Sun Microsystems, Inc. may make improvements and/or changes in the product(s) and/or the program(s) described in this publication at any time.

The authors and publisher have taken care in the preparation of this book, but make no expressed or implied warranty of any kind and assume no responsibility for errors or omissions. No liability is assumed for incidental or consequential damages in connection with or arising out of the use of the information or programs contained herein.

The publisher offers excellent discounts on this book when ordered in quantity for bulk purchases or special sales, which may include electronic versions and/or custom covers and content particular to your business, training goals, marketing focus, and branding interests. For more information, please contact:

U.S. Corporate and Government Sales
(800) 382-3419
corpsales@pearsontechgroup.com

For sales outside the United States, please contact:

International Sales
international@pearson.com

Visit us on the Web: informit.com/ph

Library of Congress Cataloging-in-Publication Data:

Cade, Mark.

Sun Certified Enterprise Architect for Java EE study guide / Mark Cade, Humphrey Sheil. — 2nd ed.

p. cm.

Previous ed.: Sun Certified Enterprise Architect for J2EE technology study guide, 2002.

ISBN 978-0-13-148203-6 (pbk. : alk. paper) 1. Electronic data processing personnel—Certification. 2. Java (Computer program language)—Examinations—Study guides. I. Sheil, Humphrey. II. Cade, Mark. Sun Certified Enterprise Architect for J2EE technology study guide. III. Title.

QA76.3.C23 2010

005.13'3—dc22

2009052010

ISBN-13: 978-0-13-148203-6
ISBN-10: 0-13-148203-3

Text printed in the United States on recycled paper at RR Donnelley in Crawfordsville, Indiana
First printing February 2010

I dedicate this book to my lovely wife Lara for putting up with all the long hours. Your support, compassion, and love drove me to finish this book. I look forward to a wonderful vacation to make up for the time spent on this book.
—Mark Cade

I wish the reader of this book the very best toward passing the SCEA exam, and in the process, becoming a better architect. Better architects create better designs and code—and that's what we all strive to do.
—Humphrey Sheil

Contents

Chapter 3 **Web Tier Technologies. 35**

Acknowledgments

Mark wishes to thank all of his past colleagues who have been great sounding boards in developing material for creating architectures.

Humphrey would like to thank the Java EE community, inside and outside Sun Microsystems, for building and growing the JEE platform to where it is today. A rich, vibrant programming platform needs good design leadership to take it forward, and that is what the SCEA certification, and this book, strives to engender.

The authors would also like to thank all those who provided great feedback to help improve this book, including Ken Saks and Chris Herron.

About the Authors

Mark Cade is a lead developer and assessor for the Sun Certified Enterprise Architect for Java EE exam. He has more than 20 years of experience as a software engineer and has extensive experience creating architectures for Java EE solutions for Fortune 500 companies. He worked at the Sun Microsystems Java Center as a Senior Java Architect until 2006. He is currently employed at BigFix.

Humphrey Sheil is a lead developer and assessor for the Sun Certified Enterprise Architect for Java EE exam. With a background specializing in enterprise architecture and integration in the United States and Europe, he holds a M.Sc. and B.Sc. in Computer Science from University College Dublin. He is currently the CTO at Comtec Group.

CHAPTER 1

What Is Architecture?

Introduction

The Sun Certified Enterprise Architect exam is comprised of three parts: knowledge-based multiple choice, assignment, and questions that each requires a short essay answer. You must pass all three parts in order to complete your certification.

Each subsequent chapter in this book will follow the same basic structure. The chapter starts with a listing of the exam objectives that are described in the chapter, followed by a "Prerequisite Review" section, which identifies any assumed knowledge for the chapter and provides other reading material to acquire the assumed knowledge. A "Discussion" section, which describes the topics in the chapter with a focus on the exam objectives, is next. This is followed by "Essential Points," which is a summary of the key ideas in the chapter. Finally, the "Review Your Progress" section focuses on questions that might appear on the exam.

This first chapter will lay the groundwork for an understanding of how the exam developers define architecture and some common terminology. Having this understanding will help you in each of the subsequent chapters.

Prerequisite Review

This book assumes a certain level of knowledge for the readers. If you do not have the prerequisite knowledge, you must gain this knowledge elsewhere before proceeding with this book. Each chapter will have a list of prerequisite knowledge for the objectives covered in that chapter. This set of prerequisites covers the entire book:

- You understand object-oriented concepts, such as encapsulation, inheritance, polymorphism, and interfaces.
- You have programmed in an objected-oriented language, preferably the Java programming language.
- You have designed object-oriented programs and systems.
- You are using this book to prepare for the Sun Certified Enterprise Architect (SCEA) for Java Enterprise Edition Technology exam.

Becoming a full-fledged system architect requires many years of real-world experience creating architectures and designing systems. This book is not a substitute for that experience, but a study guide to assist you on your path to become a Sun Certified Enterprise Architect for Java Enterprise Edition (JEE) technology. As a study guide, it will make assumptions about knowledge you should have and only cover the key details for the exam.

Discussion

The best starting point for this book is to make sure that you are on the same page as the exam developers. Having this common vocabulary will reduce confusion in the later chapters. A clear and concise definition of architecture is imperative to your success on this exam. Once you understand the definition, you must understand your role in creating architecture. You must realize what your tasks are. Finally, you must understand the purpose of creating architecture. You create architecture to support the service-level requirements of a system. Without service-level requirements, your systems cannot meet customer demand for availability, reliability, and scalability. These service-level requirements keep a company from having a "CNN" moment, which occurs when the failure of your computer systems makes headline news on CNN.

Understanding Architecture

According to the Rational Unified Process:

Software architecture encompasses the significant decisions about the organization of a software system. The selection of the structural elements and their interfaces by which the system is composed together with their behavior as specified in the collaboration among those elements. The composition of the structural and behavioral elements into progressively larger subsystems, the architectural style that guides this organization, these elements, and their interfaces, their collaborations, and their composition. Software architecture is concerned not only with structure and behavior but also with usage, functionality, performance, resilience, reuse, comprehensibility, economic and technology constraints and trade-offs, and aesthetic issues.[1]

That is a lengthy definition, so let's look at a simpler definition provided by the SunTone Architecture Methodology:

Architecture is a set of structuring principles that enables a system to be comprised of a set of simpler systems each with its own local context that is independent of but not inconsistent with the context of the larger system as a whole.[2]

Both definitions focus on system structure. You create architecture to describe the structure of the system to be built and how that structure supports the business and service-level requirements. You can define the structure of a system as the mechanisms that the system employs to solve the common problems of the system. A mechanism is a capability that supports the business requirements in a consistent and uniform manner. For example, persistence is a mechanism that should be used consistently throughout the system. This means that, any time the system uses persistence, it is handled in the same manner. By defining persistence as an architectural mechanism, you provide a default method of addressing persistence that all designers should follow and implement consistently. The architectural mechanisms—such as persistence, distribution, communication, transaction management, and security—are the infrastructure on which you build the system and must be defined in your architecture.

---

[1] Philippe Kruchten, *The Rational Unified Process: An Introduction, Third Edition* (Upper Saddle River, NJ: Addison-Wesley Professional, 2003).

[2] Sun Microsystems, Inc.

What does it mean to create architecture? It means that you have created a software infrastructure that addresses the service-level requirements that have been identified for the system. For example, if the system has a service-level requirement that states no user response time will be greater than three seconds, the software infrastructure you create must ensure that the system can meet this requirement. It also means that you have given the designers an infrastructure that allows them to design and code the system without worrying about compromising this service-level requirement. One of the real issues around architecture is: When does the creation of an architecture stop and the design process begin? There is not a definitive answer for every system. This issue of architecture and design can be summed up in terms of focus and control. Architecture defines what is going to be built, and design outlines how you will build it. One or a few individuals who focus on the big picture control the architectural process, and design is controlled by many individuals who focus on the details of how to achieve the big picture. An architect creates architecture to a point where the design team can use it to make the system achieve its overall goals. So, if you are creating an architecture for experienced designers, you would not produce as much detailed documentation that you would need if you had a group of less-experienced designers.

As you create an architecture to satisfy the business and service-level requirements of a system, you usually don't have unlimited funds to purchase hardware, software and development resources, so you need to make the system work within your predefined limitations. For example, how can you make the system scale to meet the demands of the Internet age, when you have only a single computer to support your internal employees? How do you create architecture without funds to buy software products? These are examples of problems faced by architects when they are creating system architecture. You will be presented with many difficult choices and make many trade-offs to solve these types of problems when creating your architecture. As you make these trade-offs, it is important that you document each decision made regarding the architecture of the system, so developers understand why decisions were made, and you should not receive questions from developers about those trade-offs. If you make a decision to have an Oracle database persist the objects in the system, you should document why you chose Oracle over another database vendor. This allows others working on the project or entering the project at a later time to understand why decisions were made and prevents you from justifying your decision over and over again. Most of the trade-offs you make when creating architecture focus on the service-level requirements or mechanisms. Most systems do not have the funding available to meet all of the service-level requirements originally envisioned by the system stakeholders. As the architect, you must balance the service-level requirements against the cost to attain these requirements. If it will cost your entire budget to buy high-availability hardware to achieve the 24x7 availability—thereby leaving no money to purchase an application server to help maintain that service-level requirement on the software side—you must make adjustments in your software architecture. These adjustments depend on the system for which you are creating the architecture and your relationship with the stakeholders.

Role of the Architect

> The ideal architect should be a person of letters, a mathematician, familiar with historical studies, a diligent student of philosophy, acquainted with music, not ignorant of medicine, learned in the responses of jurisconsults, familiar with astronomy and astronomical calculations.
> —Vitruvius, circa 25 BC

Vitruvius was not referring to a software architect, but the basic idea is that the architect should have the following characteristics. An architect should be a person who is well rounded, mature, experienced, educated, learns quickly, a leader, communicates well, and can make the difficult decision when necessary. For architects to be well rounded, they must have a working knowledge of the business or problem domain. They can gain this knowledge through experience or education. In addition, architects must have a broad knowledge of technology. An architect might have first-hand experience with a particular technology, but he must have at least a general understanding of competing technologies to make informed decisions about which technology can work best. A good architect evaluates all possible solutions to a problem regardless of the technology being used.

What does the architect do? How is an architect different from a senior developer? These are some of the common questions that get asked over and over again in the industry. We will explain, from the exam developer's point of view, these questions so you have that common understanding when taking the exam. The designer is concerned with what happens when a user presses a button, and the architect is concerned with what happens when ten thousand users press a button. An architect mitigates the technical risks associated with a system. A technical risk is something that is unknown, unproven, or untested. Risks are usually associated with the service-level requirements and can occasionally be associated with a business requirement. Regardless of the type of risk, it is easier to address the risks early in the project while creating architecture, than to wait until the construction phase of the project, when you have a large developer base that could potentially be waiting while you are solving risks.

An architect must lead the development team to ensure that the designers and developers build the system according to the architecture. As the leader, difficult decisions must be made about trade-offs in the system, and the architect is the person who must make those decisions. To lead the project team, the architect must be a good communicator, both written and oral. It is up to the architect to communicate the system to the designers and developers who will build it. This is typically done with visual models and group discussions. If the architect cannot communicate effectively, the designers and developers will probably not build the system correctly.

More Detail on the Exam Itself

Having considered the role and responsibilities of the architect, we now move on to consider the exam itself. The exam is composed of three main parts, as follows:

- **Part I: The multiple choice segment**—Designed to test your knowledge of all aspects of the JEE platform.
- **Part II: The assignment**—Designed to test your ability to construct a JEE-based solution to a defined business problem.
- **Part III: The essay questions**—Designed to test your ability to both critique and defend design decisions in your solution.

Now let's dive into each part in more detail.

Part I: Multiple Choice

In Part I of the exam, the candidate must sit and pass a multiple choice format exam. Each candidate is presented with 64 questions, and these questions are in turn drawn from a much larger bank of questions to ensure that each candidate experiences a wide variety of questions.

Here is some interesting (we hope!) background on these questions. They were written during the summer of 2007 in Broomfield, Colorado, by a team of about ten practicing Java architects. The questions are tied *specifically* to the Java Enterprise Edition 5 platform edition. This means that a new set of questions will be developed for future JEE edition releases, and you should always be mindful of the specific JEE release for which you are preparing to take the certification.

The facilitator for the workshop in Broomfield laid out some central tenets that informed how the questions were constructed, namely the following:

- **No trick questions**—The candidate must be able to read the question and understand exactly what knowledge is being tested by that question.
- **Do not test "learning by rote"**—Other exams in the Java curriculum require detailed knowledge of API footprints, method signatures, and return types. This exam does not; rather, the questions test the candidates ability to display high-level knowledge about the JEE platform and how the components relate to each other, and the best way to apply the JEE platform to solve a given business problem.

So, even in Part I of the exam—before you get your teeth into the main assignment in Part II—the exam tests your ability to evaluate multiple technology options to a business problem, and to use the information given in the question stem, to select the *best* answer. From an exam technique perspective, you should apply the normal time management practices to Part I. Simply put, you have 64 questions to answer in a fixed time period; therefore, you need to ensure that you devote an appropriate amount of time to each question.

The questions that comprise Part I are drawn from all sections of the exam remit, namely the following:

- Application Design Concepts and Principles
- Common Architectures (mainly two, three, and n-tier)
- Integration and Messaging (JMS and web services)
- Business Tier Technologies (EJBs—session, entity, JPA, and MDBs)
- Web Tier Technologies (JSP, JSF, Servlets, and so on)
- Applicability of Java EE Technology (selecting the best JEE implementation for a short business scenario)
- Design Patterns (drawn from the Gang of Four book and the JEE patterns book)
- Security (both the core Java platform and the JEE security capabilities)

Omitting any of these sections in your revision schedule is not recommended. One of Part I's primary goals is to test your broad knowledge of the JEE platform, and you are guaranteed to face questions on all of these sections.

For ease of reference, this book is built around the exact same structure as the exam objectives themselves. Also, at the end of each chapter, we provide questions of the same complexity and difficulty as you can expect to find in the exam, along with fully worked answers, so that you can see the logic employed by the examiners.

Part II: Solving the Business Problem

On successful completion of Part I of the exam, you will receive a download link for Part II of the exam. The assignment pack details the business problem that you have been allocated; just like Part I, the assignment will be drawn from a wider pool so that the entire body of candidates does not receive the same assignment. The assignment does not self-destruct after reading, nor will solving it bring you into contact with attractive potential partners (short- and long-term) or introduce you to a glamorous, jet-setting lifestyle. On a positive note, however, it will make you a better architect and is an important step in closing in on the JEE certification.

Part II requires a decent investment of time—somewhere between 25 and 35 hours on average. The deliverables of Part II are as follows. (This text is taken from the exam assignment itself and is identical no matter which scenario you are allocated.)

It is your task to create an architecture and design for the System under Discussion (SuD) with the given business domain model, information provided above, and requirements in the use cases. The architecture must be built using the JEE platform. All deliverables will be accepted as HTML only and each diagram must be UML compliant.

1. Create a class diagram for the SuD. Public method names referenced in other UML diagrams (for example, sequence diagrams) should be provided.
2. Create a component diagram for the SuD showing the components used in the system and their interaction. Examples of components are EJBs, Servlets, JSPs, major POJOs (Plain Old Java Objects), and important Managers/Controllers/Design Pattern implementations.
3. Create a deployment diagram that describes the proposed physical layout of the major tiers of the SuD.
4. Create either a sequence or collaboration diagram for each use case provided.

In addition to these UML deliverables, the exam requires you to

1. List the top three risks and identify a mitigation strategy for each risk.
2. List any assumptions made during the process of coming up with the architecture and design.

Your architecture and design will be graded on how well it supports the requirements detailed in this document and on the clarity of all information provided in both textual and diagrammatic form.

The general feedback from candidates is that these deliverables/requirements are clear and unequivocal. Nevertheless, candidates do often stray from this list, resulting in a poor or even a failing score for Part II. In Chapter 9, "Tackling Parts II and III," we document and work through a complete Part II assignment in detail in order to show a fully worked solution of the expected standard.

Part III: Defending Your Solution

Once Part II has been completed and the solution uploaded for grading, you will then be asked to answer eight questions on your Part II solution. These questions are very different to the questions that comprise Part I.

They are not multiple choice; rather, they require a short paragraph (on average, between 150 and 250 words per answer) of English text that answers the question posed.

The questions test your knowledge about your Part II submission, in three important respects:

- That all design decisions have advantages and disadvantages and need to be considered in context.
- That you understand the fundamental non-functional requirements (NFRs) that impact all business systems and can articulate how your solution meets these NFRs. Indicative examples include performance, scalability, reliability, security, and availability.
- That you can articulate why you believe the chosen and can document alternatives considered, as well as reasons for rejecting those alternatives.

The Part III questions are straightforward and to the point. They probe your level of understanding of JEE and your solution. Many candidates find it tempting to provide curt, one-line (in some cases, just one word) answers or to state that the question is answered elsewhere. Avoid this temptation and provide well-constructed answers to each question posed, aiming for a response length of between 150 and 200 words. If your written English skills are poor, practice writing generic answers to the NFRs listed previously in advance. As long as the examiner can understand your answer, marks will not be deducted for poor English.

Preparing for the Exam

Most people who buy this book do so because they want a study roadmap to help prepare them for the exam. Providing that roadmap has influenced this book a great deal. Let's now work through how we believe the book should be used as an aid in preparing for the exam.

Preparing for Part I

Part I of the exam is covered in Chapters 2 through 8 of this book. The main content of each chapter details the areas of the objective that we believe are most important and warrant explicit attention in the book. The start of each chapter details the resources that we believe contain the best information on the specific objective and also that were used by the Part I question authors to generate the questions (and answers) themselves.

Preparing for Part II

Read Chapter 9 because we provide a sample assignment of the same complexity and detail that you can expect to receive in the exam itself. We then step through each of the required deliverables of Part II, showing how each deliverable is created from the information contained in the assignment itself.

Preparing for Part III

Chapter 9 also covers Part III of the exam. We review the proposed solution to the sample assignment, detailing how it addresses basic non-functional requirements, such as scalability, security, and performance.

Essential Points

- The role of the architect is to make the designers and developers productive as quickly as possible.
- The role of the architect is to make the development team productive as soon as possible by communicating the essential structure of the system.
- The exam consists of three main sections: multiple choice, a worked assignment, and essay questions on the solution.
- This book covers all three parts—each chapter addresses Part I as the chapters mirror the exam objectives, whereas Chapter 9 specifically covers Parts II and III.

Review Your Progress

There are no specific questions in the exam for this chapter. This chapter lays the groundwork for the rest of this book and gives you insight into the thinking of the exam developers.

CHAPTER 2

Architecture Decomposition

- Explain the main advantages of an object-oriented approach to system design, including the effect of encapsulation, inheritance, and use of interfaces on architectural characteristics.

- Describe how the principle of "separation of concerns" has been applied to the main system tiers of a Java EE application. Tiers include client (both GUI and web), web (web container), business (EJB container), integration, and resource tiers.

- Describe how the principle of "separation of concerns" has been applied to the layers of a Java EE application. Layers include application, virtual platform (component APIs), application infrastructure (containers), enterprise services (operating system and virtualization), compute and storage, and the networking infrastructure layers.

- Explain the advantages and disadvantages of two-tier, three-tier, and multi-tier architectures when examined under the following topics: scalability, maintainability, reliability, availability, extensibility, performance, manageability, and security.

Introduction

This chapter will explain the decomposition of the larger system into smaller components and advantages and disadvantages of decomposing by tiers and/or layers. The major theme of architecture is the decomposition of the larger system into smaller components that can be built in relative isolation, as well as provide for the service-level requirements:

13

scalability, maintainability, reliability, availability, extensibility, performance, manageability, and security.

Prerequisite Review

This chapter assumes that you are already familiar with the following:

- Object-oriented concepts, such as encapsulation, inheritance, and use of interfaces

Discussion

Most architects do not follow a methodical approach to decomposition; they typically approach decomposition in a haphazard fashion. They may use a little layering and a little coupling and cohesion, but not really understand why they choose the approaches they did. We present a set of decomposition strategies that can be applied in a methodical fashion to assist with your system decomposition.

Decomposition Strategies

Decomposition can be broken down into ten basic strategies: layering, distribution, exposure, functionality, generality, coupling and cohesion, volatility, configuration, planning and tracking, and work assignment. These ten strategies can be grouped together, but not all ten are applied in any given architecture. For any strategies that are grouped together, you choose one of the strategies and then move on to the next grouping. Here are the groups:

- **Group 1**—Layering or Distribution
- **Group 2**—Exposure, Functionality, or Generality
- **Group 3**—Coupling and Cohesion or Volatility
- **Group 4**—Configuration
- **Group 5**—Planning and Tracking or Work Assignment

Grouping the strategies in this manner enables you to combine strategies that are related and will not be typically applied together. For example, if you are to decompose by layering, you will not typically decompose by distribution as well. You will notice that the groups are also ordered so that the last decomposition strategy is by Planning or Work Assignment. You would not start decomposing your system by Work Assignment and then move to Functionality.

Layering

Layering decomposition is some ordering of principles, typically abstraction. The layers may be totally or partially ordered, such that a given layer x uses the services of layer y, and x in turn provides higher-level services to any layer that uses it. Layering can be by layers or tiers, as explained later in the chapter. Layering is usually a top-level decomposition and is followed by one of the other rules.

Distribution

Distribution is among computational resources, along the lines of one or more of the following:

- Dedicated tasks own their own thread of control, avoiding the problem of a single process or thread going into a wait state and not being able to respond to its other duties.
- Multiple clients may be required.
- Process boundaries can offer greater fault isolation.
- Distribution for separation may be applied, perhaps with redundancy, for higher reliability.

Distribution is a primary technique for building scalable systems. Because the goals and structure of process/threads is often orthogonal to other aspects of the system, it typically cuts across many subsystems and is therefore often difficult to manage if it is buried deep in a system's structure. More often than not, if you decompose by layering, you will not decompose by distribution and vice versa.

Exposure

Exposure decomposition is about how the component is exposed and consumes other components. Any given component fundamentally has three different aspects: services, logic, and integration. **Services** deals with how other components access this component. **Logic** deals with how the component implements the work necessary to accomplish its task. **Integration** deals with how it accesses other components services.

Functionality

Functionality decomposition is about grouping within the problem space—that is, order module or customer module. This type of decomposition is typically done with the operational process in mind.

Generality

Generality decomposition is determining whether you have a reusable component that can be used across many systems. Some parts of a system are only usable within the existing system, whereas other parts can be used by many systems. Be careful not to make assumptions that a component may be used by another system in the future and build a reusable component for a requirement that does not exist yet.

Coupling and Cohesion

Coupling and Cohesion decomposition, as in low coupling and high cohesion, is keeping things together that work together (high cohesion), but setting apart things that work together less often (low coupling).

Volatility

Volatility decomposition is about isolating things that are more likely to change. For example, GUI changes are more likely than the underlying business rules. Again, be careful not to make assumptions that are not documented in requirements, as this can create a complex system.

Configuration

Configuration decomposition is having a target system that must support different configurations, maybe for security, performance, or usability.

It's like having multiple architectures with a shared core, and the only thing that changes is the configuration.

Planning and Tracking

Planning and Tracking decomposition is an attempt to develop a fine-grained project plan that takes into account ordering dependencies and size. **Ordering** is understanding the dependencies between packages and realizing which must be completed first. A good architecture will have few, if any, bi-directional or circular dependencies. **Sizing** is breaking down the work into small-enough parts so you can develop in a iterative fashion without an iteration taking several months.

Work Assignment

Work Assignment decomposition is based on various considerations, including physically distributed teams, skill-set matching, and security areas. As an architect, you need to anticipate and determine composition of teams for design and implementation.

To start the decomposition process, you would select a decomposition strategy from group 1 and determine if you have decomposed the architecture sufficiently for it to be built. If not, then you move to group 2 and select a strategy for decomposition and evaluate the architecture again. You continue to decompose using a strategy from each group if it applies until you have the system broken down into small-enough components to start building. Something else to keep in mind during your decomposition is the notion of tiers and layers.

Tiers

A **tier** can be logical or physical organization of components into an ordered chain of service providers and consumers. Components within a tier typically consume the services of those in an "adjacent" provider tier and provide services to one or more "adjacent" consumer tiers.

Traditional tiers in an architecture are client, web/presentation, business, integration, and resource.

Client

A client tier is any device or system that manages display and local interaction processing. Enterprises may not have control over the technologies available on the client platform, an important consideration in tier structuring. For this reason, the client tier should be transient and disposable.

Web

Web tiers consist of services that aggregate and personalize content and services for channel-specific user interfaces. This entails the assembly of content, formatting, conversions, and content transformations—anything that has to do with the presentation of information to end users or external systems. These services manage channel-specific user sessions and translate inbound application requests into calls to the appropriate business services. The web tier is also referred to as the presentation tier.

Business

Business tier services execute business logic and manage transactions. Examples range from low-level services, such as authentication and mail transport, to true line-of-business services, such as order entry, customer profile, payment, and inventory management.

Integration

Integration tier services abstract and provide access to external resources. Due to the varied and external nature of these resources, this tier often employs loosely coupled paradigms, such as queuing, publish/subscribe communications, and synchronous and asynchronous point-to-point messaging. Upper-platform components in this tier are typically called "middleware."

Resource

The resource tier includes legacy systems, databases, external data feeds, specialized hardware devices such as telecommunication switches or factory automation, and so on. These are information sources, sinks, or stores that may be internal or external to the system. The resource tier is accessed and abstracted by the integration tier. The resource tier is also referred to as the data tier.

Layers

A **layer** is the hardware and software stack that hosts services within a given tier. Layers, like tiers, represent a well-ordered relationship across interface-mediated boundaries. Whereas tiers represent processing chains across components, layers represent container/component relationships in implementation and deployment of services. Typical layers are application, virtual platform, application infrastructure, enterprise services, compute and storage, and networking infrastructure.

Application

The application layer combines the user and business functionality of a system on a middleware substrate. It is everything left after relegating shared mechanisms (middleware) to the application infrastructure layer, lower-level general purpose capabilities to the enterprise services layer, and the enabling infrastructure to the compute and storage layer. The application layer is what makes any particular system unique.

Virtual Platform (Component APIs)

The virtual platform layer contains interfaces to the middleware modules in the application infrastructure layer. Examples of this layer include the component APIs, such as EJBs, Servlets, and the rest of the Java EE APIs. The application is built on top of the virtual platform component APIs.

Application Infrastructure (Containers)

The application infrastructure layer contains middleware products that provide operational and developmental infrastructure for the application. Glassfish is an example of a container in the application infrastructure. The virtual platform components are housed in an application infrastructure container.

Enterprise Services (OS and Virtualization)

The enterprise services layer is the operating system and virtualization software that runs on top of the compute and storage layer. This layer provides the interfaces to operating system functions needed by the application infrastructure layer.

Compute and Storage

The compute and storage layer consists of the physical hardware used in the architecture. Enterprise services run on the compute and storage layer.

Networking Infrastructure

The networking infrastructure layer contains the physical network infrastructure, including network interfaces, routers, switches, load balancers, connectivity hardware, and other network elements.

Service-Level Requirements

In addition to the business requirements of a system, you must satisfy the service-level or quality of service (QoS) requirements, also known as non-functional requirements. As an architect, it is your job to work with the stakeholders of the system during the inception and elaboration phases to define a quality of service measurement for each of the service-level requirements. The architecture you create must address the following service-level requirements: performance, scalability, reliability, availability, extensibility, maintainability, manageability, and security. You will have to make trade-offs between these requirements. For example, if the most important service-level requirement is the performance of the system, you might sacrifice the maintainability and extensibility of the system to ensure that you meet the performance quality of service. As the expanding Internet opens more computing opportunities, the service-level requirements are becoming increasingly more important—the users of these Internet systems are no longer just the company employees, but they are now the company's customers.

Performance

The performance requirement is usually measured in terms of response time for a given screen transaction per user. In addition to response time, performance can also be measured in transaction throughput, which is the number of transactions in a given time period, usually one second. For example, you could have a performance measurement that could be no more than three seconds for each screen form or a transaction throughput of one hundred transactions in one second. Regardless of the measurement, you need to create an architecture that allows the designers and developers to complete the system without considering the performance measurement.

Scalability

Scalability is the ability to support the required quality of service as the system load increases without changing the system. A system can be considered scalable if, as the load increases, the system still responds within the acceptable limits. It might be that you have a performance measurement of a response time between two and five seconds. If the system load increases and the system can maintain the performance quality of service of less than a five-second response time, your system is scalable. To understand scalability, you must first understand the capacity of a system, which is defined as the maximum number of processes or users a system can handle and still maintain the quality of service. If a system is running at capacity and can no longer respond within an acceptable time frame, it has reached its maximum scalability. To scale a system that has met capacity, you must add additional hardware. This additional hardware can be added vertically or horizontally. Vertical scaling involves adding additional processors, memory, or disks to the current machine(s). Horizontal scaling involves adding more machines to the environment, thus increasing the overall system capacity. The architecture you create must be able to handle the vertical or horizontal scaling of the hardware. Vertical scaling of a software architecture is easier than the horizontal scaling. Why? Adding more processors or memory typically does not have an impact on your architecture, but having your architecture run on multiple machines and still appear to be one system is more difficult. The remainder of this book describes ways you can make your system scale horizontally.

Reliability

Reliability ensures the integrity and consistency of the application and all its transactions. As the load increases on your system, your system must continue to process requests and handle transactions as accurately as it did before the load increased. Reliability can have a negative impact on scalability. If the system cannot maintain the reliability as the load increases, the system is really not scalable. So, for a system to truly scale, it must be reliable.

Availability

Availability ensures that a service/resource is always accessible. Reliability can contribute to availability, but availability can be achieved even if components fail. By setting up an environment of redundant components and failover, an individual component can fail and have a negative impact on reliability, but the service is still available due to the redundancy.

Extensibility

Extensibility is the ability to add additional functionality or modify existing functionality without impacting existing system functionality. You cannot measure extensibility when the system is deployed, but it shows up the first time you must extend the functionality of the system. You should consider the following when you create the architecture and design to help ensure extensibility: low coupling, interfaces, and encapsulation.

Maintainability

Maintainability is the ability to correct flaws in the existing functionality without impacting other components of the system. This is another of those systemic qualities that you cannot measure at the time of deployment. When creating an architecture and design, you should consider the following to enhance the maintainability of a system: low coupling, modularity, and documentation.

Manageability

Manageability is the ability to manage the system to ensure the continued health of a system with respect to scalability, reliability, availability, performance, and security. Manageability deals with system monitoring of the QoS requirements and the ability to change the system configuration to improve the QoS dynamically without changing the system. Your architecture must have the ability to monitor the system and allow for dynamic system configuration.

Security

Security is the ability to ensure that the system cannot be compromised. Security is by far the most difficult systemic quality to address. Security includes not only issues of confidentiality and integrity, but also relates to Denial-of-Service (DoS) attacks that impact availability. Creating an architecture that is separated into functional components makes it easier to secure the system because you can build security zones around the components. If a component is compromised, it is easier to contain the security violation to that component.

Impact of Dimensions on Service-Level Requirements

As you are creating your architecture, and from a system computational point of view, you can think of the layout of an architecture (tiers and layers) as having six independent variables that are expressed as dimensions. These variables are as follows:

- Capacity
- Redundancy
- Modularity
- Tolerance
- Workload
- Heterogeneity

Capacity

The capacity dimension is the raw power in an element, perhaps CPU, fast network connection, or large storage capacity. Capacity is increased through vertical scaling and is sometimes referred to as height.

Capacity can improve performance, availability, and scalability.

Redundancy

The redundancy dimension is the multiple systems that work on the same job, such as load balancing among several web servers. Redundancy is increased through horizontal scaling and is also known as width.

Redundancy can increase performance, reliability, availability, extensibility, and scalability. It can decrease performance, manageability, and security.

Modularity

The modularity dimension is how you divide a computational problem into separate elements and spread those elements across multiple computer systems. Modularity indicates how far into a system you have to go to get the data you need.

Modularity can increase scalability, extensibility, maintainability, and security. It can decrease performance, reliability, availability, and manageability.

Tolerance

The tolerance dimension is the time available to fulfill a request from a user. Tolerance is closely bound with the overall perceived performance.

Tolerance can increase performance, scalability, reliability, and manageability.

Workload

The workload dimension is the computational work being performed at a particular point within the system. Workload is closely related to capacity in that workload consumes available capacity, which leaves fewer resources available for other tasks.

Workload can increase performance, scalability, and availability.

Heterogeneity

The heterogeneity dimension is the diversity in technologies that is used within a system or one of its subsystems. Heterogeneity comes from the variation of technologies that are used within a system. This might come from a gradual accumulation over time, inheritance, or acquisition.

Heterogeneity can increase performance and scalability. It can decrease performance, scalability, availability, extensibility, manageability, and security.

Common Practices for Improving Service-Level Requirements

Over the years, software and system engineering practices have developed many best practices for improving systemic qualities. By applying these practices to the system at the architecture level, you can gain a higher level of assurance for the success of the system development.

Introducing Redundancy to the System Architecture

Many infrastructure-level practices for improving systemic qualities rely on using redundant components in the system. You can apply these strategies to either the vendor products or the server systems themselves. The choice depends primarily on the cost of implementation and the requirements, such as performance and scalability.

Load Balancing

You can implement load balancing to address architectural concerns, such as throughput and scalability. **Load balancing** is a feature that allows server systems to redirect a request to one of several servers based on a predetermined load-balancing algorithm. Load balancing is supported by a wide variety of products, from switches to server systems, to application servers. The advantage of load balancing is that it lets you distribute the workload across several smaller machines instead of using one large machine to handle all the incoming requests. This typically results in lower costs and better use of computing resources. To implement load balancing, you usually select a load-balancer implementation based on its performance and availability. Consider the following:

- **Load balancers in network switches**—Load balancers that are included with network switches and are commonly implemented in firmware, which gives them the advantage of speed.
- **Load balancers in cluster management software and application servers**—Load balancers that are implemented with software are managed closer to the application components, which gives greater flexibility and manageability.
- **Load balancers based on the server instance DNS configuration**—Load balancer is configured to distribute the load to multiple server instances that map to the same DNS host name. This approach has the advantage of being simple to set up, but typically it does not address the issue of session affinity.

Load balancers also provide a variety of algorithms for the decision-making component. There are several standard solutions from which to choose, as follows:

- **Round-robin algorithm**—Picks each server in turn.
- **Response-time or first-available algorithm**—Constantly monitors the response time of the servers and picks the one that responds the quickest.
- **Least-loaded algorithm**—Constantly monitors server load and selects the server that has the most available capacity.
- **Weighted algorithm**—Specifies a priority on the preceding algorithms, giving some servers more workload than others.

- **Client DNS-based algorithm**—Distribute the load based on the client's DNS host and domain name information.

In addition to these solutions, most load-balancer implementations enable you to create your own load-balancing strategy and install it for use. Your selection of a load-balancing strategy is largely based on the type of servers you are managing, how you would like to distribute the workload, and what the application domain calls for in performance. For example, if you have equally powerful machines and a fairly even distribution of transaction load in your application, it would make little sense to use a weighted algorithm for load balancing. This approach could result in an overloaded system that might fail. An equal distribution of workload would make more sense.

Failover

Failover is another technique that you can use to minimize the likelihood of system failure. **Failover** is a system configuration that allows one server to assume the identity of a failing system within a network. If, at any point in time, a server goes down due to overloading, internal component failure, or any other reason, the processes and state of that server are automatically transferred to the failover server. This alternative server then assumes the identity of the failed system and processes any further requests on behalf of that system. One important aspect of failover is available capacity, which can be handled in two ways:

- **Designing with extra capacity**—If you design a server group with extra capacity, all the systems work for you, but at low usage levels. This means that you are spending money on extra computing resources that will not be used under normal load and operation conditions.

- **Maintaining a stand-by server**—If you design a server group to have a stand-by server, you are spending money on a system that does no work whatsoever, unless (or until) it is needed as a failover server. In this approach, the money spent on unused computing resources is not the important thing to keep in mind. Instead, you should view the expenditure as insurance. You pay for the stand-by server and hope that you will never have to use it, but you can rest easier knowing that the stand-by server is there in case you ever need it.

Clusters

Clusters also minimize the likelihood of system failure. A **cluster** is a group of server systems and support software that is used to manage the server group. Clusters provide high availability to system resources. Cluster software allows group administration, detects hardware and software failure, handles system failover, and automatically restarts services in the event of failure.

The following cluster configurations are available:

- **Two-node clusters (symmetric and asymmetric)**—A configuration for which you can either run both servers at the same time (symmetric), or use one server as a stand-by failover server for the other (asymmetric).

- **Clustered pairs**—A configuration that places two machines into a cluster, and then uses two of these clusters to manage independent services. This configuration enables you to manage all four machines as a single cluster. This configuration is often used for managing highly coupled data services, such as an application server and its supporting database server.

- **Ring (not supported in Sun Cluster 3.0 Cool Stuff software)**—A configuration topology that allows any individual node to accept the failure of one of its two neighboring nodes.

- **N+1 (Star)**—A configuration that provides N independent nodes, plus 1 backup node to which all the other systems fail over. This system must be large enough to accept the failover of as many systems as you are willing to allow to fail.

- **Scalable (N-to-N)**—A configuration that has several nodes in the cluster, and all nodes have uniform access to the data storage medium. The data storage medium must support the scalable cluster by providing a sufficient number of simultaneous node connections.

Improving Performance

The two factors that determine the system performance are as follows:

- **Processing time**—The processing time includes the time spent in computing, data marshaling and unmarshaling, buffering, and transporting over a network.

- **Blocked time**—The processing of a request can be blocked due to the contention for resources, or a dependency on other processing. It can also be caused by certain resources not available; for example, an application might need to run an aggressive garbage collection to get more memory available for the processing.

The following practices are commonly used to increase the system performance:

- Increase the system capacity by adding more raw processing power.
- Increase the computation efficiency by using efficient algorithms and appropriate component models technologies.

Introduce cached copies of data to reduce the computation overhead, as follows:

- Introduce concurrency to computations that can be executed in parallel.
- Limit the number of concurrent requests to control the overall system utilization.
- Introduce intermediate responses to improve the performance perceived by the user.

To improve the system throughput, it is common that a timeout is applied to most of the long-lasting operations, especially those involving the access to an external system.

Improving Availability

The factors that affect the system availability include the following:

- **System downtime**—The system downtime can be caused by a failure in hardware, network, server software, and application component.
- **Long response time**—If a component does not produce a response quick enough, the system can be perceived to be unavailable.

The most common practice to improve the system availability is through one of the following types of replication, in which redundant hardware and software components are introduced and deployed:

- **Active replication**—The request is sent to all the redundant components, which operate in parallel, and only one of the generated responses is used. Because all the redundant components receive the same request and perform the same computation, they are automatically synchronized. In active replication, the downtime can be short because it involves only component switching.

- **Passive replication**—Only one of the replicated components (the primary component) responds to the requests. The states of other components (secondary) are synchronized with the primary component. In the event of a failure, the service can be resumed if a secondary component has a sufficiently fresh state.

Improving Extensibility

The need for extensibility is typically originated from the change of a requirement. One of the most important goals of the architecture is to facilitate the development of the system that can quickly adapt to the changes. When you create the architecture, consider the following practices for the system extensibility:

- **Clearly define the scope in the service-level agreement**— Scope change is one of the most common reasons for project failure. Defining a clear scope is the first step to limiting unexpected changes to a system.

- **Anticipate expected changes**—You should identify the commonly changed areas of the system (for example, the user interface technology), and then isolate these areas into coherent components. By doing this, you can prevent ripple effects of propagating the change across the system.

- **Design a high-quality object model**—The object model of the system typically has an immediate impact on its extensibility and flexibility. Therefore, you should consider applying essential object-oriented (OO) principles and appropriate architectural and design patterns to the architecture. For example, you can apply the MVC pattern to decouple the user interface components from the business logic components.

Improving Scalability

You can configure scalability in the following two ways:

- **Vertical scalability**—Adding more processing power to an existing server system, such as processors, memory, and disks (increase the height of the system). Sometimes, replacing an existing server with a completely new but more capable system is also considered vertical scaling.

- **Horizontal scalability**—Adding additional runtime server instances to host the software system, such as additional application server instances (increase the width of the system).

Vertically scaling a system is transparent to system architecture. However, the physical limitation of a server system and the high cost of buying more powerful hardware can quickly render this option impractical. On the other hand, horizontally scaling a system does not have the physical limitation imposed by an individual server's hardware system.

Another consideration you must take into account is the impact that horizontal scaling has on the system architecture. Typically, to make a system horizontally scalable, not only do you need to use a software system that supports the cluster-based configuration, but you also need to design the application such that the components do not depend on the physical location of others.

Tiers in Architecture

Let's conclude this chapter talking about how tiers impact the service-level requirements. When most of the industry is talking about tiers in an architecture, they are referring to the physical tiers such as client, web server, and database server. An architecture can have multiple logical tiers, as we previously mentioned, and still be deployed in a two-tier architecture. With the advent of virtualization, the physical deployment is not as critical as it was years ago. Virtualization enables you to have what are perceived as physical tiers on the same physical machine. You could be running the web server and application server on the same physical hardware just in different operating systems, so physical tiers are not as important as the logical tiers and the separation of concerns.

When talking about two-tier, three-tier, or n-tier, the client tier is usually not included unless explicitly stated, as in two-tier client/server.

Two-Tier Systems

Two-tier systems are traditionally called client/server systems. Most two-tier systems have a thick client that includes both presentation and business logic and a database on the server. The presentation and business logic were typically tightly coupled. You could also have a browser-based two-tier system with business logic and database on the same server.

Advantages

Security is an advantage as most of these systems are behind the corporate firewall, so most security breaches are the result of physical security breaking down and non-employees using an unsecured PC. Performance is usually pretty good unless the company uses extremely old laptops that have minimal memory.

Disadvantages

Availability is a disadvantage because if one component fails, then the entire system is unavailable. Scalability is a problem, as the only component you can increase is the database. In order to add new functionality in a two-tier system, you will definitely impact the other components—therefore, extensibility fails. Manageability is problematic, as it becomes almost impossible to monitor all the PCs that are running the client code. Maintainability has the same problem as extensibility.

Reliability is not really an advantage or disadvantage in a two-tier system. As the load increases, more requests will be coming to the database, and most databases will be able to handle the increased transaction throughput unless it is already at capacity.

Three- and Multi-Tier Systems

Three-tier systems are comprised of web, business logic, and resources tiers. Multi-tier systems have web, business logic, integration, and resource tiers. They share the same advantages and disadvantages when it comes to non-functional requirements.

Advantages

Scalability is improved over a two-tier system as you move the presentation logic away from the client PC onto a server that can be clustered. Availability is also improved with the ability to cluster tiers and provide failover. Extensibility is improved because functionality is separated into different tiers. You could modify presentation with minimal to no impact to the business logic. The same is true for maintainability. Manageability is greatly improved because the tiers are deployed on servers, making it easier to monitor the components. Separating the tiers allows for more points to secure the system, but be careful that you do not impact performance.

Performance could be an advantage or disadvantage. Primarily, it is an advantage, as you can spread out the processing over many servers, but it can become a disadvantage if you have to transfer large amounts of data between the servers.

Disadvantages

Multi-tier systems are inherently more complex, but when it comes to the "ilities," there are no real disadvantages to have a multi-tier system. With that said, just because you have multiple tiers does not mean you have a great architecture. Just remember to not overdo the number of tiers.

Essential Points

- A basic rule of thumb is any time you add a tier, scalability, availability, extensibility, manageability, maintainability, reliability, security, and performance improve. There is, of course, a law of diminishing returns that states that at some point, more tiers will degrade performance, availability, and reliability as there are far more points of failure.

- Architecture is a set of structuring principles that enables a system to be comprised of a set of simpler systems, each with its own local context that is independent of but not inconsistent with the context of the larger system as a whole.[1]

- Scalability is the ability to support the required quality of service as the system load increases without changing the system.
- Reliability ensures the integrity and consistency of the application and all of its transactions.
- Availability ensures that a service/resource is always accessible.
- Extensibility is the ability to add additional functionality or modify existing functionality without impacting the existing system functionality.
- Maintainability is the ability to correct flows in the existing functionality without impacting other components of the system.
- Manageability is the ability to manage the system to ensure the continued health of a system with respect to scalability, reliability, availability, performance, and security.
- Security is the ability to ensure that the system cannot be comprised.

Review Your Progress

These questions test your understanding of multi-tier architectures and their most appropriate use to solve a given business problem:

1. Your web design company is designing web sites for all the retail stores in a local mall. Your company must create a consistent "look and feel" for the sites. Once this "look and feel" project has gone through demonstration, enhancement, and approval with the mall's clients, your job is complete, and the development of the actual B2C system will be handled by a different company.

---

[1] Sun Microsystems, Inc.

Which architecture is most appropriate for your prototype project?

A. Three-tier, application-centric

B. Three-tier, enterprise-centric

C. Three-tier, web-centric

D. Two-tier, web-centric

Answer: D. Because it is a prototype, you only need two-tiers. This enables you to do it quickly and focus on your part of the system, which is the user interface.

2. A company has an existing system that is a two-tier (presentation/business logic → database) architecture, which requires installation of code on a PC. The company wants the system to support thin clients (browser).

   Which three non-functional requirements will be improved as a result of separating the business logic into a third-tier (presentation → business logic → database)? (Choose three.)

   A. Security

   B. Extensibility

   C. Performance

   D. Manageability

   E. Maintainability

   Answers: B, D, E. There are no guarantees that security or performance will be improved. The system will be more extensible, as you could add more business logic without impact to presentation. Manageability will be improved because you could monitor the business tier, and maintainability will be improved because you could have different programmers working on what they do best.

CHAPTER 3

Web Tier Technologies

- State the benefits and drawbacks of adopting a web framework in designing a Java EE application.
- Explain standard uses for JSPs and Servlets in a typical Java EE application.
- Explain standard uses for JSF components in a typical Java EE application.
- Given a system requirements definition, explain and justify your rationale for choosing a web-centric or EJB-centric implementation to solve the requirements. Web-centric means that you are providing a solution that does not use EJBs. An EJB-centric solution will require an application server that supports EJBs.

Introduction

This chapter covers the area of presentation in the JEE platform, and focuses on presentation technologies designed to render in a standards-compliant HTML browser. In addition to focusing on the presentation specifications and technologies that are included in the JEE platform, we go one step further and analyze the benefits and drawbacks of using a web framework to lend additional structure to a web application (whether it also uses EJB or not) at the expense of additional complexity or runtime overhead.

Prerequisite Review

The following list details resources and specifications that you should be familiar with before reading this chapter. The main resources are as follows:

- **The JavaServer Pages 2.1 specification**—JSR 245
- **The Servlet 2.5 specification**—JSR 154
- **The JSF 1.2 specification**—JSR 252
- **The JSTL 1.2 specification**—JSR 52
- **The Java EE 5 specification**—JSR 244

We now cover the specific topics that should be addressed at a high level before more esoteric and advanced discussions on the relative advantages and disadvantages of the various JEE web tier technologies.

Model View Controller (MVC)

Regardless of application domain or industry vertical, technology platform, and client-side technology, everyone agrees that three fundamental concepts should be decoupled and kept separate—namely, the data, the business logic that operates on that data, and the presentation of that data to the end user (see Figure 3-1). In the JEE platform, the seminal design pattern that enforces this separation of concerns is called the MVC model. In the earliest releases of the specification, references were made to Model 1 and Model 2 architectures. However, all mainstream frameworks now embrace Model 2 exclusively—where views (implemented as JSP pages with or without JSF components) forward to a central controller (implemented as a Servlet), which invokes a named handler for the page or action before forwarding the user to a well-defined page to render the outcome of the request.

Web Container

The web container is analogous to the EJB container described in Chapter 4, "Business Tier Technologies." Simply put, one of the biggest advantages of the JEE platform is how much it gives the developer out of the box from an infrastructure perspective, leaving the developer free to focus on how to use the JEE platform to implement the required business logic for their application. A web container provides services to presentation and control components provided by the developer, implemented as JSPs, JSF components, Servlets, filters, web event listeners, and plain old Java classes (POJOs). These services include concurrency control, access to user-managed transactions (more on this later), configuration, and security management.

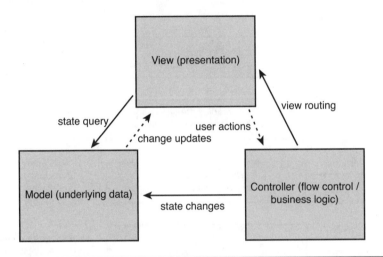

Figure 3-1   A high-level schematic depicting the basic flow between the three major components of the Model-View-Controller design pattern. All MVC web frameworks follow this basic separation of concerns to a greater or lesser extent.

Servlets

A Servlet is a server-side component designed to handle inbound service requests from remote clients. Although the vast majority of all Servlets implemented are designed to respond to HTTP/HTTPS GET and POST requests, the Servlet model is designed to accommodate any protocol that is predicated around a request/response model. Servlet developers must implement the `javax.servlet.Servlet` interface, and specifically for HTTP Servlet developers, the `javax.servlet.HttpServlet` interface. The core service method contains the routing logic that forwards the inbound request to the appropriate handler. A Servlet is hosted by the container, and multiple threads use it in order to provide a scalable system unless the developer explicitly chooses not to do this by implementing the `SingleThreadedModel` tagging interface. (This interface has been deprecated, as it results in systems that do not scale.) Figure 3-2 illustrates the Servlet lifecycle, as managed by the web container.

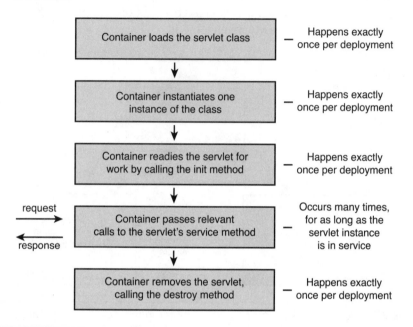

Figure 3-2   The Servlet lifecycle is quite simple, as opposed to that of other server-side components in the JEE stack. Most developers simply override three methods— `init()`, `doGet()`/`doPost()`, and `destroy()` to add required behavior.

Filters

Filters are server-side components hosted by the web container that receive an inbound request *before* it is received by any other component. Filters then are used to pre-process requests—for example, log the event, perform security checks, and so on. Filters are frequently used by web frameworks to make their operation as transparent to the developer as possible, removing or at least ameliorating a significant barrier to their adoption—the complexity (perceived or otherwise) of their development overhead. In addition, filters can be used to perform dedicated processing after a request has been received and processed.

Listeners

Listeners are server-side components hosted by the web container that are notified about specific events that occur during a Servlet's lifecycle. Listeners are used to take actions based on these events. The event model is well-defined, consisting solely of notifications on the web context (Servlet initialization and destruction, attribute adds/edits/deletes) and session activity (creation, invalidation and timeout, and attribute adds/edits/deletes).

JavaServer Pages (JSP)

JavaServer Pages are HTML pages with embedded mark-up that is evaluated at runtime by the web container to create complete HTML pages, which are sent to the client for rendering to the end user. JSP technology has matured significantly in the JEE platform—key elements added since its inception have been the JSTL (Java Standard Tag Library) and the Unified Expression Language (EL), which are covered in separate sections later in the chapter. However, from an architect's perspective, their purpose is simple—they represent the ongoing effort from Sun to enforce a workable MVC model in the JEE, separating presentation logic from business logic. Like all container-managed objects in the JEE, JSPs have a well-defined lifecycle, depicted in Figure 3-3.

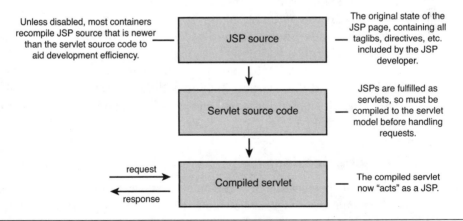

Figure 3-3 Although JSPs appear more complex than Servlets, and represent a huge improvement on developer productivity and code maintainability, they are actually implemented as Servlets under the hood by the web container.

Java Standard Tag Library (JSTL)

The JSTL is a set of tag libraries that forms part of the JSP specification. Before the advent of the JSTL, open source communities such as Apache, commercial companies, and indeed individual software teams built their own tag libraries. The JSTL brought much needed standardization to the tag library space, allowing developers and architects to effectively delegate control and enhanced presentation logic tags to the specification writers and focus instead on their application logic. The JSTL is an example of open standards adding tangible value to developers as the JSP specification grows out to bring structure to an area badly needing it.

Unified Expression Language (EL)

The EL was introduced in the JSP 2.0 specification, whereas the JSF 1.1 specification introduced its own EL. The word *Unified* indicates that in JEE 5, these two EL definitions come together in a logical attempt to simplify the overall platform. Simply put, the addition of an EL provides developers with the ability to banish Java scriptlets from JSP pages completely. There are two constructs to represent EL expressions: ${expr} and #{expr}. $ indicates that the expr is evaluated immediately, whereas # indicates to the container that evaluation should be deferred. The container also makes a number of useful implicit objects available to an executing EL snippet—for example, requestScope, sessionScope, and so on. Access to this information further improves the ability of EL to replace custom Java snippets in JSP. Custom Java snippets on their own are not necessarily a bad thing (although the code is often more readable, elegant, and easier to maintain). The single biggest danger when developers need to code Java in JSPs is that they implement not only presentation logic, but business logic as well, violating the core tenet of the MVC design pattern.

Managing Sessions

The Servlet specification provides an elegant way to allow a client-server conversation to manage session state over the HTTP protocol, which is essentially stateless. The web container provides access to a simple map, called the HttpSession, where developers can read from and write to any data that needs to be stored in order to process a client's request. Judicious use of this object is needed, however—storing large objects, such as collections of search results, is a known performance and scalability anti-pattern.

JavaServer Faces (JSF)

JavaServer Faces is a UI framework for web applications based on the JEE platform. Initially controversial (and still so in some quarters), with many developers and architects resenting the imposition of yet another web framework in an already over-crowded space, JSF has grown to represent the foremost method of constructing web UIs as recommended by Sun Microsystems. Nevertheless, many application architects still eschew JSF and use a simpler MVC model, typically leveraging a web framework like vanilla Struts.

Disregarding any good or bad will toward JSF, let's examine its goals. JSF is designed to be easy to use by developers; it is also designed to allow developers to stop thinking in terms of HTTP requests and responses and instead to think about UI development in terms of user- and system-generated events. JSF components are re-usable, improving developer productivity, software quality, and system maintainability; the clear intent of the JSF specification is that the technology be toolable, or provided with deep and mature support from IDEs like Eclipse, Netbeans, and IntelliJ. In this respect, JSF maps closely onto other technologies like ASP.NET from Microsoft and, in turn, is a clear break with directions from frameworks like Ruby on Rails, where the developer is never far away or insulated from the underlying HTTP request/response model.

Templating Frameworks

Especially in the early days of JSP and even today, a segment of the developer and architect population railed against what they saw as the poor ease of development and runtime performance provided by the JSP-centric model. These malcontents fought back against the tide by using the Servlet container to build out a simpler, more efficient way of including dynamic content in HTML fragments, resulting in the creation of template-centric frameworks such as Velocity and FreeMarker. The presence of these frameworks has kept the JSP and JSF communities honest, in showing how simple web development can and should be. However, no matter how relevant or pressing the claims of these frameworks may be, the fact remains that the mandated way to build presentation logic in the JEE platform is either using JSP or JSF.

Web Frameworks

Web frameworks fill the gap between the JSP/Servlet/JSF specification and what an architect needs in order to build a consistent, high-quality web application in the UI platform. The authors are often struck, after reading a three- or four-hundred-page specification, how many open questions there are. In the case of web UIs, a good web framework fills that void, providing the architect and developer with a clear roadmap on exactly how to implement core features such as action handlers, client- and server-side validation, how to handle transactions in a sensible manner, integrate security, manage session state, and build a maintainable and understandable web UI. In fact, mainstream web frameworks have been so successful, a significant percentage of architects have decided not to use EJB in their applications at all—so confident are they that a good web framework is all that is needed to design and construct a good JEE system. And in many, if not most, cases, they are correct. EJBs in the JEE platform provide specific features that are necessary only when business requirements dictate it (these features are detailed in Chapter 4, along with the decision matrix governing when the use of EJBs is appropriate). If you choose not to specify or use a web framework in Part II of the exam, be prepared to clearly justify your decision. We believe that very few, if any, non-trivial Java projects are not using a web framework to impose standard practices on the development team, to produce maintainable code, and to avoid re-inventing the wheel on every new development.

Discussion

In this section, we examine the best uses for each of the various components of the JEE web technology stack. Almost all the components can be used to tackle any presentation/flow control/business logic problem, but the specifics of JSPs, Servlets, JSF, and so on mean that they each are better-suited to specific scenarios, as detailed here.

JSPs and Servlets—Standard Uses

JSPs handle the presentation of data to the end user. They should contain no business logic. A good rule of thumb is to minimize or eliminate entirely all Java code from JSPs and replace it instead with either

EL, the JSTL, or a custom/third-party tag. This guideline tends to reinforce the role of JSPs as the V in MVC—that is, the View.

JSF—Standard Uses

The standard uses for JSF are the same as for JSP. As an architect, you are faced with a choice: either continue to use JSP with JSTL and a good MVC framework, or use JSF. They do the same thing. Also, they are not mutually exclusive. It is perfectly possible to add tags to a JSP page that represent a specific JSF UI component, resulting in a hybrid solution. JSF garnered a significant amount of bad press when it first launched (as have many 1.0 implementations of specifications in the JEE platform), but it has matured since then. Many architects, however, simply see no need for it and prefer JSP with JSTL and EL.

Web-Centric Implementations

As intimated earlier, a significant proportion (exact figures are not available and indeed vary by industry vertical) of all JEE applications in existence today are deployed using only a web container—that is, they do not use EJBs. This class of JEE application is termed web-centric.

The current version of the exam tests this concept in detail. As a JEE architect, you are perfectly entitled to stipulate that EJBs not be used in your design, but you must clearly understand why that decision is mandated and the impact of that decision on your developers as they implement the business logic. The exam tests this concept by presenting you with a set of scenarios. Scenarios that have a strong messaging, transaction, or security management component are all candidates where an EJB-centric implementation is warranted and indeed necessary. (Let's be blunt—choosing EJB is the right answer.) Scenarios where ease of development is key, where an existing application is already web-centric, or where transactions are not key to the business (read-only or read-mostly) mean that you should choose a web-centric answer from those provided in the exam.

There are some stand-out reasons where using EJB is simply not warranted. The most straight-forward example is a standard Create, Read, Update, and Delete (CRUD) application built using Struts to organize and control the presentation and business logic tiers, and Hibernate plus a DAO access layer to implement the persistence tier. Assuming that there are no asynchronous messaging requirements or

JMS queues or topics to access, and that the functionality contained in the web container for concurrency control, security, and session management is sufficient, then the right decision is to adopt a web-centric approach.

Now, let's consider an alternative scenario. You work for XYZ Bank, a large multinational bank with investment and retail operations, which has invested significant amounts of capital into a transactional system based on mainframe technology over the last thirty years. Ensuring system reliability and security are paramount; there is absolutely no room for data corruption from edge conditions, such as the lost update or optimistic locking going wrong. If the system enters into an unknown state because of a technology failure, not only will the system need to be brought back within 10 minutes in order to avoid a service-level agreement (SLA) breach, the relevant regulatory authorities must also be notified and a full system audit will be enforced. As the solution architect, do you believe that using only the web container segment of the JEE platform is sufficient to meet the non-functional requirements detailed here?

We would answer this rhetorical question as follows: It is possible to fulfill the preceding scenario using only a web framework, but we would not be comfortable in doing so. Many aspects of the EJB framework lend themselves very well to this type of deployment; choosing to use only a web framework will essentially force you, as the architect, into replicating in your code the reliability and availability characteristics that already exist in the core JEE platform. This is not a good use of your time and will result in a buggier implementation that needs to be maintained moving forward.

EJB-Centric Implementations

Let's reconsider the bank scenario laid out in the previous section. Looking at the business requirements, we can see that they translate into non-functional requirements (NFRs) focusing on system correctness, reliability, and security. In this scenario, and answering the question posed in the last section, assuming that the internal bank systems can be accessed by a non-EJB solution, it is possible to achieve a solution that will meet the NFRs using only a web-centric solution. But, and this is the key point, you will need to commit your team to writing entire modules of custom code to replace features that you get from an EJB container for free. In addition, it is likely that you will also need to take advantage of vendor-specific libraries/mechanisms to implement these modules. That is the key point. In the scenarios examined here, there is no right or wrong answer—just more correct and less correct. And that is the key role of an architect: to examine the possible solutions and select the most correct solution, taking into account the vagaries of the known set of business requirements.

Rationale for Choosing Between EJB-Centric and Web-Centric Implementations

As you may have gathered from the two preceding sections, neither we, nor indeed the exam, believe that a web-centric or an EJB-centric architecture is always right or always wrong. The decision to select one over the other is based purely on an impassionate review of the facts relating to a specific project. In order of decreasing importance, the pertinent facets to consider are as follows:

- Transaction requirements—The more onerous, the bigger the reason to select EJB.
- Security requirements—Again, the more onerous, the bigger the reason to select EJB.
- Messaging requirements—Need to integrate with an asynchronous messaging system—Again, if present, a clear reason to select message-driven beans (MDBs); that is, the EJB-centric approach.
- Performance.
- Ease of development.
- Scalability.
- Existing team skills or existing project implementation.

The last four facets listed are not reasons in themselves that will conclusively force you to choose one approach over the other; indeed, the waters have been muddied in recent JEE releases for each. The primary focus for EJB 3.0 (and continued in 3.1) is improving the ease of development. As you will see in Chapter 4, the general consensus is that EJBs are now, at last, easy enough to develop that their use is warranted in situations where previously system designers did not specify their use. Assuming an efficient container implementation, stateless session beans should be as efficient as Servlets/Action handlers in executing business logic on the server side as a proxy for the client. The obvious exception here is stateful session beans. The need to maintain one session bean per connected client for the duration of the conversation will always make stateful session beans a poor scaling design choice, suitable only for a small subset of applications with very specific requirements.

The Future of Client-Server Communication

It is worth noting that the current release of the exam was written in 2007 and contains material on Asynchronous JavaScript and XML, or AJAX. Architects must understand the benefits of AJAX as they relate to providing an enhanced end-user experience and how the JEE 5 platform allows server-side components to service AJAX requests from browsers. Looking forward, the exam will be refreshed in sympathy with the release of future JEE versions. If JEE 6 or 7 is released into a world where AJAX is declining in favor of cometd (HTTP continuations), or another way of enhancing the end-user experience for browser-based applications, then expect that technology to be reflected in the questions posed. After all, the exam is written by a team of subject matter experts who construct the questions and answers for Part I based on the current state of play in the Enterprise Java space.

Essential Points

- Presentation tier technologies remain a major element of the JEE 5 platform and are a significant source of exam content for Parts I and III.

- Part II is less concerned with the actual presentation technology selected (within reason, of course) and more concerned with the candidate displaying two things—in-depth understanding of the business requirements and selecting a presentation technology that meets those requirements.

- JSF has grown from the presentation tier that disgruntled architects tried to ignore to a significant element of the JEE platform—and for the exam. If you are a JSP-centric architect, beef up on JSF because you need to know it.

■ The exam tests your understanding of the best UI technologies to use in the JEE platform by presenting a series of scenarios. The description of the scenario provides all the information you need to select the correct technology/combination of technologies to use from the multiple choice answers provided.

■ In the real world, there are no official "Sun recommended" blueprint patterns—only guidelines and recommendations. As a JEE architect, one of your key skills is the ability to analyze application requirements and choose the best combination of JEE technologies—especially at the web tier—to meet those requirements, while not over-engineering the solution.

Review Your Progress

These questions test your understanding of JEE web components and their most appropriate use to solve a given business problem:

1. You are the architect at a large investment bank. Your main area of responsibility is a new web application designed to replace the aging user interface for the existing clearing house back office system. One of the systems is read from/written to via a JMS Queue in asynchronous fashion and transactions and security management are paramount. Select the most appropriate implementation from the following list:

   A. JSP and JSTL accessing a business logic tier built using EJBs and MDBs.
   B. JSP and JSTL accessing a business logic tier built using MDBs only.
   C. JSF accessing the systems directly.
   D. JSP accessing the systems directly.

   Answer: A. B is not flexible enough, omitting EJBs and allowing only MDBs. C and D couple the presentation tier directly to the backend resource, creating potential security, performance, and maintenance problems. A provides what is needed.

2. You are the architect at ACME Corporation—the hottest Internet start-up of the moment. The start-up provides a front-end accessible by multiple devices, from smart phones to desktops, and provides innovative social networking features to its members. The key considerations for the system are performance and scalability, and individual messages between members are not considered important (that is, they can be resent). Select the most appropriate implementation for this system from the following list:

   A. JSP + JSTL accessing the messaging layer directly.
   B. JSF accessing EJBs, with access to the messaging layer mediated by a JMS client and MDB.
   C. JSF accessing stateful session beans—one for each connected client.
   D. JSP + JSTL accessing a JPA-based persistence tier.

   Answer: A. All of the other options contain a reasonable chance that there will be an unnecessary overhead associated with the components used—EJBs, JPA, and so on. A is the simplest answer for the business problem described, especially when the priority of performance and scalability is stated in the stem of the question.

3. You are a subject matter expert on JEE consulting for ACME Corporation. ACME has an existing application built using an earlier version of the JEE platform. Performance and scalability are not an issue, although system is not as maintainable as ACME would like. The application uses JSP pages as part of a Model 2 MVC architecture with Java code in the JSPs and some presentation coded as Servlets. What do you recommend?

   A. A complete rewrite of the existing presentation architecture to leverage JSF and JPA.
   B. A deeper analysis of the current system to ensure that JEE best practices (especially the MVC model) are respected throughout the code, replacing Java code in JSPs with JSTL and EL as necessary and making Servlets act purely as controllers.
   C. ACME move the system to use Ruby on Rails.

D. A complete rewrite of the current architecture to leverage JSF, session beans, JMS, and JPA.

Answer: B. All of the other answers are nonsensical when you realize where ACME is. They have a system that works today, which requires some refactoring to move to MVC, and they simply need a roadmap after this work is completed to guide them onto JEE 6, 7, and beyond. No rewrites are necessary.

4. You are a JEE architect at ABC Bank and have been tasked with designing their next-generation UI framework for online banking. The online banking application must be accessible by both standard browser clients and mobile devices. What do you recommend as the simplest and most optimal solution?

   A. A JSF-based architecture, leveraging the capability of device or channel-specific JSF renderers to support both mobile and standard browser clients.
   B. A JSP-only architecture, with custom logic to probe and handle individual devices at runtime.
   C. A Servlet-based architecture.
   D. A template-based architecture.

   Answer: A. JSF is designed to support exactly this type of use case—the other available options, while workable, are not the most optimal or most simple.

5. XYZ Corp has retained you as the architect for their latest web application: XYZOnline. This application allows customers to search, browse, and order catalog content online. XYZOnline accesses the inventory and payment systems as web services. What architecture do you recommend?

   A. JSP/JSF pages accessing the web services layer using stateless session beans.
   B. Servlets accessing the web services directly using JAX-WS as necessary.
   C. JSP/JSF pages accessing the web services layer using JAX-WS as necessary.
   D. JSP/JSF pages accessing the web services using JMS.

Answer: C. A uses stateless session beans when nothing in the description warrants their usage. B uses Servlets to generate the presentation, while D uses JMS in the wrong context. C is the best solution for the stated business requirements.

6. You have been asked to evaluate multiple web presentation technologies for ABC Corp. Their priorities are future-proofing, tooling support from IDEs and the ability to render multiple versions of the same component for different devices. What do you recommend to ABC?

   A. Use JSF components as part of a Servlet.
   B. Use JSTL and the EL as part of JSP pages.
   C. Use JSF components as part of JSP pages.
   D. Use JSTL and the EL as part of Servlets.

   Answer: C. The key to choosing C is to realize that the question guides you there by mentioning tooling support and future proofness. B is close but does not match the requirements exactly. D and A are not valid answers.

CHAPTER 4

Business Tier Technologies

- Explain and contrast uses for entity beans, entity classes, stateful and stateless session beans, and message-driven beans and understand the advantages and disadvantages of each type.

- Explain and contrast the following persistence strategies: Container Managed Persistence (CMP), BMP, JDO, JPA, and ORM, and using Data Access Objects (DAOs) and direct JDBC-based persistence under the following headings: ease of development, performance, scalability, extensibility, and security.

- Explain how Java EE supports the deployment of server-side components implemented as web services and the advantages and disadvantages of adopting such an approach.

- Explain the benefits of the EJB3 development model over previous EJB generations for ease of development, including how the EJB container simplifies EJB development.

Introduction

This chapter addresses probably the single biggest component of the Java Enterprise Edition platform: Enterprise Java Beans, or EJBs. EJBs have evolved significantly from the earliest versions of the platform and, in particular, in this release of the platform, integrating as it does the EJB 3 specifications. As a matter of fact, this chapter deals with the subject matter that has changed most between JEE 5 and earlier revisions—no other chapter in this book (or objective in the exam objectives list) explicitly calls out knowledge of how one specification version number has changed the platform. The expert group behind the revised exam objectives and content felt strongly enough that EJB 3 represented a major step forward, and warranted explicit attention both by the exam and the exam candidate.

Prerequisite Review

The following list details resources and specifications that you should be familiar with before reading this chapter. Make no mistake—the EJB specifications are long and boring, and a significant percentage is intended to be read by the container developers; nevertheless, they must be read and understood by anyone who wants to pass the exam. Your knowledge of EJBs is tested in multiple sections of Part I and clearly has an influence on your implementation decisions and justifications for the same in Parts II and III:

- The EJB 3.0 specification (all three parts that the specification is composed of: ejbcore, persistence, and simplified): Java Specification Request (JSR) 220.
- Chapter 5, "Integration and Messaging" (to understand JMS and how message-driven beans are used to interact with this technology).
- The Java EE 5 specification: JSR 244.

We note that there are many objective and subjective opinions and articles available on the web relating to EJB. We also note that knowledge of this material is not required reading by the successful exam candidate. Although this comment is certainly intended to be tongue in cheek, it is also 100% accurate and correct. The exam does not test your knowledge of how good or bad earlier EJB specifications were or how good or bad implementations that use EJB are over non-EJB implementations (or vice versa). You are simply expected to display an advanced/expert level of knowledge of how to use EJBs to solve a given business problem in the most correct way. Your subjective opinion, and that of thousands of other commentators, is irrelevant. Your ability to form an objective and logical opinion and use it to choose the right answer, or most appropriate implementation, is what counts.

You are not expected to learn the EJB specification by rote (in total, the three parts add up to over 1,000 pages), but you are expected to know the major characteristics of EJB and why you would or would not use them to solve a given business problem and be able to justify and defend your decision.

As in previous and future chapters, it is not our place to describe subject matter material in detail because this would simply duplicate the resources listed in this section. However, we note the most important components and characteristics of EJBs to act as a quick cheat sheet for you.

Enterprise Java Bean

An Enterprise Java Bean (referred to as EJB from now on) is a server-side component used in JEE architectures to encapsulate a specific piece of business logic. As detailed next, there are multiple different types of EJBs in the JEE platform; however, regardless of type, there are some common characteristics common to all EJBs, as follows:

- They are distributed components—that is, they represent a unit of logically related work in an Enterprise Java application that can be accessed either locally or remotely.
- A common contract with EJB clients and EJBs is enforced by a set of well-defined interfaces.
- They are implemented as Java classes.
- They are managed at runtime by the EJB container, with the container providing important services such as transaction management, security, and concurrency control to the EJBs under its management.
- They do not explicitly manage either inbound or outbound data—the container manages all client access.
- They are configured using a combination of metadata annotations, deployment descriptors, and container-supplied variables.
- If written to use only those services defined by the EJB specification, they can be ported with minimal effort to run on other EJB containers.

In early versions of the JEE platform and in their interpretation by architects, the overall importance of EJBs was overstated, resulting in applications that were over-complex and over-engineered for the business requirement. Since then, the onus has been on architects to stipulate the use of EJBs only when a specific requirement demands it.

Although different annotations are used to define the major types of EJB, the overall EJB component model allows the following high-level characteristics:

- A stateless service, including the ability to act as a web service end point.
- A stateful service.
- A service invoked asynchronously by a separate component.
- An entity object—that is, a component that interfaces with a data store to persist an object representation of a domain object.

We now move on to consider the major types of EJB that exist in the JEE platform.

Session Bean

Session beans are EJBs that contain business logic—specifically, business logic relating to the implementation of a workflow or process. They can be considered as server-side proxies for the client. There are two specific types of session bean: stateless and stateful.

Stateless Session Bean

As their name implies, stateless session beans maintain no internal client-specific state across separate client invocations. Although this simplified programming model means that an application using stateless session beans must implement state elsewhere, there is a significant upside in that the application's scalability is improved significantly. A small (relative to the size of the number of concurrent requests) pool of stateless session beans can be used to service a significantly larger number of concurrent requests. Finally, stateless session beans register once with the EJB Timer Service to receive event notifications by adding an @Timeout annotation. Stateless session beans are the simplest of all the EJB types, as Figure 4-1 illustrates.

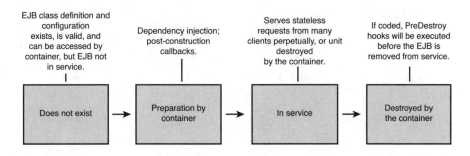

Figure 4-1 As illustrated here, the basic lifecycle of a stateless session bean is quite simple.

Stateful Session Bean

Although many behavior and lifecycle differences exist between stateless and stateful session beans, there is one crucial distinction: the ability of stateful session beans to maintain internal conversational state across multiple invocations from the same client. The advantages and disadvantages of stateful session beans are exactly opposite to those of stateless session beans—the programming model is less restrictive and more natural. However, applications that use stateful session beans are not as scalable as an equivalent application that uses stateless session beans. Stateful session beans can be activated and passivated by the container as the demand waxes and wanes depending on the number of concurrent requests, as illustrated in the lifecycle diagram shown in Figure 4-2. Stateful session beans can also optionally implement the `javax.ejb.SessionSynchronization` interface, which enables a stateful session bean to participate in a well-defined transaction, and either commit as part of the wider transaction or roll back—because of an error encountered directly, or in response to a rollback directive from the container. Finally, unlike stateless session beans, stateful session beans cannot be registered with the EJB Timer Service.

We now move on to consider the next major type of EJB: entity beans. We do note that Java Persistence API (JPA) entities are addressed here when they are not technically EJBs; however, this treatment is chosen in order to remain consistent with the exam objectives.

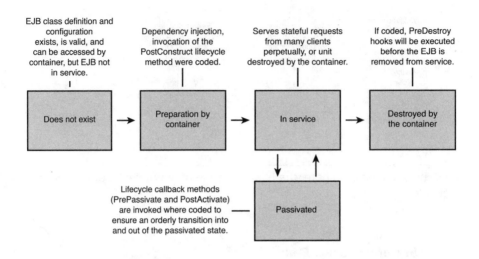

Figure 4-2 Compared to the stateless session bean lifecycle, the stateful session bean's lifecycle is more complex, but still relatively simple.

Entity Beans

Entity beans persist data. The persistence model in the latest revision of the EJB specification under scrutiny in this book (3.0) has undergone significant revision—so much so, in fact, that it has been extracted into its own mini-specification: Chapter 6 of the "ejbcore" specification now simply points the reader to the Java Persistence API reference instead. Nonetheless, entity beans as they existed in the EJB 2.1 specification must be supported by EJB 3.0-compliant containers/application servers, and they will also remain current for a long time due to their widespread usage. Therefore, they are in scope for the exam and are described here. But moving forward, it is clear that entity beans have been replaced by Java Persistence API entities (often called entity classes), and this fact should be reflected in your Part II solution—that is, there needs to be a very good reason why you would choose to use anything except entity classes in your submission. We suggest that no such reason exists.

CMP Entity Bean

Container Managed Persistence (CMP) entity beans delegate the persistence of their internal state to the container. This approach has the advantage of improving developer productivity, but control of the generated code is lost to the container; therefore, the architect must ensure that the CMP implementation of the vendor's EJB container is at least as good as the SQL code that would be generated by hand. Contrary to opinion, adopting CMP does not insulate the developers or architect from needing to know SQL or the database schema used to persist application data—these skills are still required, if only to troubleshoot the CMP implementation itself from time to time and during specific project phases (for example, performance tuning).

BMP Entity Bean

Bean Managed Persistence (BMP) entity beans require developers to explicitly code how their internal state (such as data contained in instance variables) is updated to a persistent store—typically using SQL code. Although this is the most straightforward and often the most efficient method of persisting data, it does require that the developer hand-code every single aspect of data persistence. Thus, BMP entity beans are best suited to those specific scenarios where a CMP implementation is simply not capable of delivering the performance needed, or no CMP implementation exists for the persistent store being used (a home-grown pseudo-relational database, for example).

Entity Class

The entity class is a new development in the EJB 3.0 specification. An entity class is a plain old Java object (POJO) with annotations that provide a Java Persistence API (JPA) implementation information on how to update the persistent store with the values stored in the instance variables of the entity class. One of the key design goals behind the JPA (and, by extension, entity classes) is to simplify the task of persistence. (The term "lightweight" is often used with JPA, and this is intended to convey the fact that it is easy to use and develop with, not that it is lacking in features.) The design intent has borne fruit—JPA is a much simpler method of persistence than either CMP or BMP entity beans. In the lifecycle diagram shown in Figure 4-3, the EntityManager essentially plays the role of container for the entity instance, although in a less complete way. (For example, entities can exist even when completely detached from an EntityManager—something not possible in the world of session beans.)

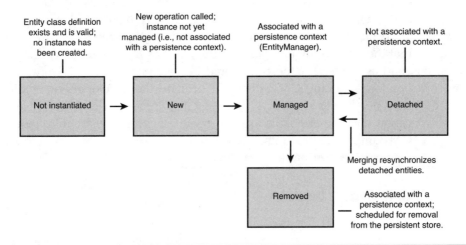

Figure 4-3 The four main lifecycle states in which an entity instance can exist (new, managed, detached, and removed) are shown here.

Persistence Strategies

In general, there are two major persistence strategies—either delegate the actual persistence to the EJB container or an Object-Relational Mapping (ORM) tool, or retain the responsibility of writing that code in return for increased control over the code and, in some cases, to generate code that is more optimal than its auto-generated equivalent. Within these two approaches, individual frameworks and design patterns have matured over time, but the high-level decision is simple: Do you want to explicitly code a persistence tier, or do you want to delegate the code to a third-party tool, providing only direction on what you want generated?

Message-Driven Bean

A message-driven bean (MDB) receives and processes messages from a JMS destination (that is, a queue or topic; see Chapter 5 for more details), thus providing the JEE platform with the capability to process messages asynchronously. MDBs are probably the simplest type of EJB (even simpler than stateless session beans) because only one method needs to be implemented: the onMessage method. More widely, MDBs can actually be used to consume messages from any Connector 1.5 resource adaptor.

Discussion

In this section, we examine the common topics of discussion that are raised when EJBs come into the frame: How much value do they really add in an architecture, how best to persist data, how to implement web services using EJBs and consume web services from EJBs, and finally, what value EJB 3 brings to the platform, compared with previous iterations of the EJB specification.

EJB Advantages and Disadvantages

The decision-making process to use or not use EJB is similar to that when considering whether or not to use a framework—you know that using the framework will impose intrinsic overheads, either at design, development, or runtime. The question is: Do the benefits of the framework outweigh the overheads for the application under consideration (System under Development [SuD])? For many application architects, the answer when evaluating EJB 1.1, 20 and 2.1 has been "no." Using EJB results in an application that takes too long to develop and runs too slowly when compared against its non-EJB counterpart. For architects practicing in some industries, however (especially financial services), the transaction management and security capabilities of the EJB container have made it mandatory since the earliest release of the platform. The advantages and disadvantages of EJB must be measured against the specific SuD.

Scalability

Using EJBs provides scalability through one key characteristic: the ability of the EJB container to manage the pool of EJBs, taking into account the number, frequency, and duration of incoming client requests (that is, the developer delegates concurrency control to the container instead of explicitly managing it). It is important to note, however, that in general, stateless session beans are far more scalable than their stateful equivalent. If the container must maintain a one-to-one relationship for M clients in the pool, then M EJBs can only ever service M concurrent clients. However, if the container can re-use stateless session beans after every method invocation, then a small number of stateless session beans in a container-managed pool can service the requirements of a significantly larger number of concurrent clients. (This is often denoted as M x N in texts.)

Security

Security is one of the core services offered to the EJB developer by the container. Along with transaction management and concurrency control, the built-in security capabilities of EJBs are one of the primary reasons for choosing to implement an architecture as EJB-centric rather than web or framework-centric. In the past, systems with a heavy and corporate-led focus on security (in particular, financial institutions) have eschewed lightweight web-centric frameworks in favor of EJB-centric architectures that provide a more fully-featured security framework. In the JEE 5 platform, however, these two things are no longer mutually exclusive, and developing with EJB 3 is now as efficient as using commonly available web frameworks.

Contrasting Persistence Strategies

Choosing how your SuD will persist data to a persistent store is another important decision, which requires multiple items to be considered and evaluated. We detail the most important of these considerations here.

Ease of Development

Approaches that abstract the developer away from explicitly coding data access and update logic are, in general, easier to develop with (as long as the tool/framework itself generates correct and efficient persistence logic). Examples of this approach include JPA and other ORM tools and CMP entity beans. By contrast, persistence approaches that require the developer to explicitly code SQL code tend to require longer development durations.

Performance

In general, the trade-off of using ORM, JPA, or CMP is that there is a runtime penalty to be paid for the productivity gains realized in the development phase. By contrast, explicit persistence strategies such as raw SQL executed via a JDBC connection take longer to develop and are more arduous to maintain, but because the developer retains full control, also represent the theoretical best-performing method of general data access and persistence. This is an esoteric point, however. A container-based persistence strategy may quite feasibly outperform a hand-crafted SQL—for example, by reducing the number of database round-trips by pre-fetching fields of related entities. Only careful, application-specific prototyping and benchmarking can recommend the right solution.

Extensibility

No data persistence approach has a clear advantage over the alternatives as far as extensibility goes. As new columns are added to tables or new business rules need to be encoded into the persistence tier, additional effort must be expended to upgrade the persistence tier to meet these new requirements. The JEE 5 specification does not explicitly address how JPA or container providers should address this requirement, so the ease of extensibility varies widely by implementation.

EJB and Web Services

We now consider how EJBs support web services to act as end points, and also how EJBs can consume data from web services to fulfill a business function.

EJBs as Web Service End Points

JEE 5 reduces the developer effort needed to expose an EJB as a web service. (This is a common theme across this release of the platform.) A developer can export all public methods on a Java class (including an EJB) simply by placing the @WebService annotation on the class definition. The platform automatically publishes the public methods of the class as web service operations, using parts of the JEE 5 platform, such as JAXB 2.0, to map the arguments for each operation into an XML schema.

EJBs Consuming Web Services

EJBs, and indeed any Java class, can access web services using the JAX-WS API (JSR 224), which forms part of the JEE 5 platform. JAX-WS replaces JAX-RPC as the primary API used to access web services in JEE applications.

Advantages and Disadvantages

The advent of JAX-WS and annotations in the JEE platform makes it trivially easy to both export EJBs as web services and to consume web services from EJBs. In general, these capabilities have the following advantages and disadvantages:

Advantages

- Developer productivity.
- Rapidly consume web services to meet new business requirements.
- Rapidly expose business logic as web services for external applications to meet new business requirements.

Disadvantages

- **Potential for a disordered application architecture**—Architects should strive for a well-defined integration layer in the architecture.
- **Potential for security concerns**—Data and information previously accessible only to authenticated users of the application is now available to external users and applications.
- **Potential for data validation to be broken or circumvented**— A previously robust component may integrate a new web service, and not check the data returned and damage the referential integrity of a database or break a business rule by using unvalidated data.

EJB 3

Since the release of the first EJB specification, there has been a vocal and growing segment of Java developers and architects who believe that it is an unproductive and bloated element of the JEE platform. Countless applications have been built using only the web technologies that make up the JEE platform (see Chapter 3, "Web Tier Technologies"), and they perform well and meet the business requirements exactly. However, stung by the criticisms leveled at earlier revisions, the EJB 3.0 expert group have revisited almost every aspect of how EJBs (of all types) are designed and developed to make them quicker, simpler, and easier to develop while still retaining all the advantages that EJBs bring to a JEE application. Let's now examine the major changes made.

Ease of Development

It is fair to say that the single biggest driver for the EJB 3.0 specification was to improve developer productivity and simplify the process of developing EJBs of all types. EJB 3.0 has succeeded in reducing the overheads traditionally associated with EJBs—a proliferation of interfaces for one component, a restrictive inheritance mechanism for the core EJB implementation class, boilerplate XML that becomes hard to keep in sync with the source code that it configures, and so on. 3.0 EJBs remove many if not all of these tiresome restrictions, giving EJBs a new lease of life in the Enterprise Java space. Whether or not these changes will encourage developers to increase their use of EJBs is a question that can only be answered in time. What we can accurately state is that previous generations of EJB specifications and implementations required a lot of extra work from the developer in return for the benefits of EJB—transaction management, concurrency control, security, and so on. The 3.0 specification and implementations of that specification reduce significantly that overhead, while still retaining all of the advantages of EJBs.

Container in EJB 3

The container in EJB 3 has not changed significantly from an architect/developer perspective. It still provides a base set of plumbing or infrastructure services, designed to allow the developer to focus on implementing the business logic for a specific application.

JPA in EJB 3

The Java Persistence API (JPA) is a significant and important step forward in the overall EJB 3.0 specification, addressing in a simpler way the core task of business data persistence that has been so complicated in previous revisions of the specification. In general, it is clear that the creators of the EJB specification believe that JPA surpasses all other methods of persistence in the JEE platform, since they have learned from existing ORM frameworks and tools, as well as mistakes made in earlier revisions of the specification. However, it is important to note that there are certain cases where JPA is not a silver bullet or panacea, specifically the following:

- **When raw performance is necessary**—That is, SQL statements need to be explicitly tuned by hand to eke out the last percentage of speed.
- **When minor modifications are being made to a persistence tier already implemented**—In this case, the benefits in rewriting the entire tier to use JPA are outweighed by the cost and risk in doing so.
- **When the underlying datastore is not well supported by mainstream JPA implementations**—For example, if the application does not persist to a relational database.

Essential Points

- The EJB component model remains a major element of the JEE 5 platform and is a significant source of exam content for all sections—I, II, and III.
- The EJB 3 specification is a major advancement on previous iterations of the EJB specification, using annotations, resource injection, and applying logical default values over configuration to improve the speed and ease of development.
- The core EJB elements are tested in the exam—why use stateless over stateful session beans, pros and cons of the available persistence strategies, commonly-applied and proven design patterns to improve EJB performance and scalability, and so on.
- In general, an architect specifies EJBs to leverage three major benefits from the EJB container: transaction management, concurrency control, and the enforcement of security, both declarative and programmatic.
- The JPA element of EJB 3.0 specifically addresses how JEE applications should address data persistence and is intended to replace classic CMP and BMP entity beans over time. However, for interoperability and backwards compatibility, an EJB 3.0-compliant container must support both JPA and EJB 2.1 entity beans.

- The JEE 5 platform makes it trivial to expose EJBs as web service end points using annotations and also for EJBs to consume web services using JAX-WS.

Review Your Progress

These questions test your understanding of EJBs and their most appropriate use to solve a given business problem:

1. You have been asked to recommend a general approach to business logic for a complex, transactional system with a 99.999% uptime requirement. What do you recommend?

   A. Use a web-centric architecture.
   B. Implement all business logic as stateful session beans.
   C. Use JPA.
   D. Use session beans with JPA as necessary to implement the business logic.

   Answer: D. Only session beans with JPA provide a transactional framework to build the application. Answer A does not apply because a web-centric approach does not intrinsically provide transactional support. The question does not specify the need for a stateful architecture; therefore, B is incorrect. Answer C does not satisfy the requirement, as JPA on its own does not provide transactional support.

2. Your application needs to read messages from a JMS queue, invoke a web service, and store the resulting response in a relational database. What type of EJB will you use as the core of the application?

   A. A stateless session bean.
   B. A stateful session bean.
   C. A message-driven bean.
   D. A CMP entity bean.

   Answer: C. All the other options may be invoked by a message-driven bean (MDB) to execute the work needed, but as the data that initiates the work arrives as a JMS message on a queue, an MDB is the only logical choice.

3. Your application will be used in a B2C high-volume environment. In general, what type of EJB do you try to avoid unless deemed absolutely necessary?

   A. Stateless session beans.
   B. Stateful session beans.
   C. Entity beans.
   D. Message-driven beans.

   Answer: B. All the other bean types have well-defined uses in multiple architectures; however, it is a widely accepted rule of thumb in the JEE architecture space to avoid the use of stateful session beans unless they are absolutely necessary because of the need to service concurrent clients in a 1..1 fashion.

4. An existing application uses EJB 2.0 CMP entity beans heavily. The application has no major issues in production, and little future development is planned. You have been asked to recommend a methodology to adopt when making minor modifications to the application. What do you recommend?

   A. JPA.
   B. BMP.
   C. CMP.
   D. Use DAO accessing JDBC directly.

   Answer: C (that is, continuing as before with no change). This question is more of a test on your pragmatic skills as an architect as opposed to your technical skills. To choose any of the other options (A, B, or D) would introduce a significant amount of new development that would need to be fully regression tested, for an application that is stable in production and has little new development planned. Note that this question deliberately engineers a situation where JPA is not the right answer!

5. XYZ Investment Bank has recently started development of a new trading system that enables users to buy and sell stocks on behalf of clients during opening hours on multiple stock exchanges worldwide. XYZ has to ensure that all system users

are treated absolutely fairly in all respects and is happy to spend whatever is needed on hardware and software to achieve that goal. What do you recommend as the best way to guarantee that each user will have his or her own dedicated resources and cannot impact each other?

A. Use CMP instead of CMP entity beans to access all resources needed by a user.

B. Use JPA instead of entity beans to access all resources needed by a user.

C. Use a JMS-based architecture with MDBs processing data to access all resources needed by a user.

D. Use stateful session beans to access and retain all resources needed by a user.

Answer: D. Only stateful session beans allow a JEE application to dedicate resources to a user for the lifetime of their session. Answers A, B, and C do not solve the core issue of ensuring that a user is treated both fairly and also has access to all resources needed. The usual argument against stateful session beans, limited system resources, is negated by the statement "…and is happy to spend whatever is needed on hardware and software to achieve that goal."

6. ABC Corp is a small B2C reverse-auctioneering online business. You have been asked to recommend a persistence strategy for their new platform, which is a green field (that is, no existing code or database schemas) project. Top priorities are ease of development and integration with EJB 3. What do you recommend?

A. JDBC.

B. CMP entity beans.

C. BMP entity beans.

D. JPA.

Answer: D. Answers A, B, and C are certainly viable and are not incorrect per se, but JPA offers the best integration with EJB 3 and has been designed with ease of development in mind. It is important to note that this question engineers a situation whereby JPA is the best option of all the options provided, despite the other options being viable in their own right, as opposed to questions that provide one clearly correct answer, surrounded with clearly incorrect answers.

7. In choosing how to model server-side components in a system design as session and entity beans, what best describes the relationship between the two EJB types?

   A. Inheritance.
   B. Separation of concerns.
   C. Common re-use principle.
   D. Scalability.

   Answer: B. Answers A, C, and D simply quote terms that apply to EJBs, but do not speak directly to the primary difference between them. Session beans act as server-side proxies for clients, and entity beans serve as components that persist state in a long-term fashion—a clear separation of concerns.

Integration and Messaging

- Explain possible approaches for communicating with an external system from a Java EE-based system given an outline description of those systems and outline the benefits and drawbacks of each approach.

- Explain typical uses of web services and XML over HTTP as mechanisms to integrate distinct software components.

- Explain how JCA and JMS are used to integrate distinct software components as part of an overall JEE application.

- Given a scenario, explain the appropriate messaging strategy to satisfy the requirements.

Introduction

In this chapter, we address an aspect that is core to almost every Java EE application in existence: how to send data to, and receive data from, another system or application. In the real world of designing, building, and managing Java EE applications, this is often a task of overriding importance, especially for large businesses with pre-existing systems. However, like all exam sections, it is no more or less important than its peers as far as the SCEA exam goes; therefore, it merits only one chapter in this book.

We review the seminal topics and specifications that you must know in order to pass the exam, before moving on to consider each in turn. Finally, we examine some sample scenarios to illustrate when one integration or messaging mechanism is more appropriate than another before providing some searching questions to test your knowledge of this particular topic.

Prerequisite Review

In order to get the most out of this chapter, you must be familiar with the following topics and resources listed here. As we state multiple times in the book, you are not required to know all the material here by rote or memorization, but equally, you cannot claim to be a proficient architect unless you understand clearly the purpose of each constituent part of the JEE 5 platform. We also cannot attempt to provide you with a structure to understand what the exam requires you to know unless you are familiar and comfortable with the subject matter. In this chapter in particular, a lot of the base material is Java and indeed JEE independent—the problem of integration and messaging has been around long before Java and affects all software architectures and programming languages. In fact, by its very nature, a significant amount of the material you will revise for this section of the exam is independent of the Java platform because it absolutely needs to be. The relevant topics and specifications (with relevant Java Specification Request, or JSR, numbers) are as follows:

- Web services, using SOAP as the messaging protocol— Independent of any Java implementations
- RESTful (Representational State Transfer) web services—Again, independent of any Java implementations or preconceptions
- Web services for Java EE 1.2 Requirements—JSR 109
- Java API for XML Web Services (JAX-WS) 2.0—JSR 224
- Java Architecture for XML Binding (JAXB) 2.0—JSR 222
- SOAP with Attachments API for Java (SAAJ) 1.3—JSR 67
- Java API for XML-based RPC (JAX-RPC) 1.1—JSR 101

- Java API for XML Registries (JAXR) 1.0—JSR 93
- Java Messaging Service (JMS) 1.1—JSR not applicable
- The Java Connector Architecture (JCA) version 1.5

We do not cover these topics/specifications in complete detail here (that would easily take up a book in its own right). However, we will cover the most seminal aspects and use cases for each, with a focus on what matters for the exam.

Web Services

A web service is a piece of software designed to allow system-to-system communication over a network. The vast majority of web services in existence today communicate using SOAP or XML over the HTTP or HTTPS protocols; however, the more general concept of a web service, as defined by the W3C, allows for multiple transport and data protocols. Web services started out as a simple concept but have since grown to encompass all the characteristics that any mature integration technology must, addressing the issues of security, reliability, and transactions through the WS-Security, WS-ReliableMessaging, WS-Coordination, and WS-AtomicTransactions specifications. As an architect, you must decide whether your application needs these additional capabilities above and beyond the WS-I Basic Profile. From an exam perspective, you must understand at a high level what each of these specifications does and how it is or is not addressed in the JEE platform.

SOAP

Simple Object Access Protocol (SOAP) is an XML-based extensible method of representing data. Web services can be written to consume and emit SOAP-based messages or XML messages. SOAP has the benefit of adding more information (via the envelope, encoding rules, and data representation conventions) over "raw XML," but the drawback of being more complex and introduces more overhead—both in terms of on-the-wire transmission size and message parsing resources. There is an ongoing battle in the web community between adherents of SOAP-centric and XML-centric messaging. You need to know both approaches and appreciate where each is more appropriate for the exam, although the exam itself has no bias toward one or the other.

WSDL

Web Services Description Language (WSDL) is a descriptor for web services, defining the information needed to access and consume a web service. Integrated development environments (IDEs) and tools from Netbeans to Eclipse to Visual Studio focus on making developer's lives easier by generating as much client/access code as possible from WSDL.

JAX-RPC

In this acronym, the JAX stem stands for Java API for XML-based, whereas the RPC stem stands for Remote Procedure Call. This API stems from an earlier revision of the Java EE specification and was created quickly to add web services support to the platform. Web services semantics were based on an older integration model known as RPC. JAX-RPC is destined for eventual deprecation and removal from the Java EE standard and has already been effectively replaced by JAX-WS. Your study of this API for the exam should focus on why JAX-WS is a better replacement for it.

JAX-WS

JAX-WS is the primary Java API for XML-based web services, both SOAP based and RESTful. As outlined previously, this API now represents the preferred way to access web services in the Java EE 5 platform and, as such, is a very important API to focus on in your revision studies. In fact, the JAX-WS specification itself states that "JAX-WS 2.0 (this specification) is a follow-on to JAX-RPC 1.1, extending it as described in the following sections." Simply using annotations such as @ WebService and @WebMethod enable developers to expose functionality as Service Endpoint Interfaces or SEIs easily. The JAX-WS API uses lower-level APIs such as JAXB, SAAJ (Soap with Attachments API for Java), JAXP (Java API for XML Parsing), and StAX (Streaming API for XML) to provide core support for basic web services to the Java EE platform—that is, the WS-I Basic Profile.

JAXB

JAXB stands for Java API for XML Binding. This API enables developers to create mappings from Java object representations to their XML equivalents (both schemas and data) and vice versa. Before JAXB, a significant percentage of integration code was devoted to the task of marshaling and un-marshaling XML data into their Java object equivalents, which was a time-consuming and error-prone development task. JAXB assumes that workload, and tries to minimize the runtime overhead of doing this over hand-crafted code. JAXB is used heavily by the main web services specification in the JEE platform: JAX-WS.

JAXR

JAXR stands for Java API for XML Registries. Like the registries themselves, this API has seen little adoption since its inception and is not an important part of the platform to focus on. Historically (going back to 2000), the vision for web services was that architects would access central repositories like UDDI using JAXR to somehow create system architectures on the fly that would meet business requirements. In fact, IBM ran an ad showing a business man switching his company's preferred widget supplier on the fly based on a web search! Time has moved on, and we know that people do business with people, not with web services. JAXR will be put out to pasture—if not in JEE 6, then certainly in JEE 7. By all means, know what it does and what its purpose is (was), but it's presence in the exam is very small.

JMS

We now move on to cover the non-web services integration elements of the Java EE platform. The Java Messaging Service (JMS) is the core messaging infrastructure used within the JEE platform to allow asynchronous Java to Java integration via queues or topics. It is technically possible to have a .NET application placing messages on a JMS queue, but most architects would favor using web services in that scenario, for reasons we will cover later in this chapter. Another way to look at JMS is as the preferred mechanism for intra-company integrations, where the architect can control both the message producer and consumer. In that scenario, JMS can provide a better solution than the main competing alternative: web services.

JMS is a very simple concept. Any Java class (the JMS client) can create a message (there are multiple types), look up via JNDI or have a reference to a JMS queue or topic (the JMS Provider) injected by the container, and then send a message, which is delivered to another JMS client that has registered with the JMS Provider. In a JEE application, message-driven beans or MDBs (see Chapter 4, "Business Tier Technologies," for more details on enterprise beans in general) are the most logical way to consume messages from a JMS Provider. Figure 5-1 illustrates the lifecycle for an MDB as managed by the container. JMS is a very important part of the exam, and you should devote serious time to it, along with web services support, when revising for Part I.

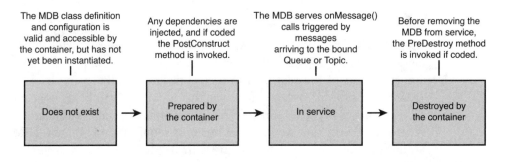

Figure 5-1   The basic lifecycle of a message-driven bean is quite simple—its sole raison d'etre is to process messages sent to its bound JMS queue or topic.

JCA

Java Connector Architecture (JCA) provides a standardized access mechanism to Enterprise Information Sources or EISs from the Java EE platform. It is fair to say that JCA is used less heavily in the real world than either web services or JMS; nevertheless, it still has its place, especially in wrapping legacy applications that still have business value and exposing their functionality as a well-formed API for consumption by Java EE applications. The need for JCA varies widely by industry; for example, Web 2.0 companies building social network applications have no need for JCA whatsoever. Financial services companies, with a substantial investment in legacy systems that still meet business requirements, use JCA widely to expose these EISs to a Java EE application server and thus lend the EIS a new lease of life.

Discussion

Integration and messaging is a wide-ranging topic, but we must attempt to impose some structure on it in order to define the problem space. We define integration as follows:

> *Integration is the process by which information is passed between two or more distinct software entities.*

That's the simplest definition we can provide. We now expand that definition by asking the following series of questions:

- Is the transfer of information synchronous or asynchronous?
- Is the transfer of information acknowledged?
- Is the transfer of information transactional?
- Does the transfer of information occur in batches composed of multiple messages or one message at a time?
- Does the transfer of information require message-level or transport-level encryption?
- Does the transfer of information occur between systems built using the same technology or different technologies?
- Does the transfer of information use a technology-specific messaging/transport protocol or a technology-independent protocol?

Asking these questions and considering the answers holistically leads the architect to select the most appropriate messaging implementation that meets the immediate business requirements. The comprehensive support for integration present in the Java EE platform (and other equivalent platforms) is a reflection of the fact that the size of the integration problem space is large—even when described simplistically using the approach adopted previously. In general, however, we can boil down a myriad of integration and messaging scenarios into a set of major scenarios that warrant further analysis.

Java to Java Integration

A substantial class of integration projects require two systems implemented on the Java platform to pass information between each other. For these projects, adopting a solution that introduces overhead in the form of a more verbose data representation or that is Java-independent is, on the face of it, only warranted if a non-Java system can be expected to also integrate with the systems currently under consideration. Nevertheless, many real-world projects use web services to integrate Java systems together, especially if the development team already has the necessary skill set. Nonetheless, there is one major component of the Java EE 5 platform that deals *precisely* with the Java to Java requirement: Java Messaging Service (JMS), which is discussed next.

Java Messaging Service (JMS)

By design, JMS is intrinsically asynchronous. Although synchronous semantics can be emulated, this goes against the design intent of JMS. JMS supports the following:

- Publish-subscribe and point-to-point messaging models.
- Message delivery acknowledgments.
- Message-level encryption.
- Distributed transactions via integration with the Java Transaction API (JTA), using the XAConnectionFactory, XAConnection, and XASession objects/interfaces.

In short, JMS is a mature and significant element of the overall platform and is treated as such in the exam.

Java to Non-Java Integration

When integrating a Java system to an external system not owned or controlled by the architect, web services are typically needed and used; JMS is not appropriate (although technically it can, and indeed has, been done) for this family of scenarios. In fact, there are two options open to the software architect using JEE: web services using SOAP or RESTful semantics and the Java Connector Architecture (JCA).

Web Services

Web services are more suitable because:

- Web services were intrinsically designed to facilitate the integration of heterogeneous systems; JMS wasn't.

- JMS is optimized for Java producers and consumers of messages.
- Using web services ensures that if the underlying implementation of the other system changes, as long as the web services contract as described in the WSDL is maintained, the other system(s) will not be impacted.
- Using web services is truly technology independent, admitting non-Java implementations as both producers and consumers of messages.

Within web services, the architect faces another decision: whether to embrace SOAP messages or to use a simpler, but less self-describing message format such as simple XML. The decision on which to use depends on the specifics of the problem at hand. Proponents of XML-RPC are proponents because of its simpler programming model, on-the-wire representation of data, and lower runtime overhead. Adherents of SOAP, on the other hand, value its total commitment to self-describing interoperability, at the expense of a steeper learning curve, more verbose representation, and higher runtime overhead to construct and parse SOAP messages than a leaner alternative. Both models are covered in the exam, as each is appropriate and valid in certain circumstances.

Java Connector Architecture (JCA)

JCA is used to provide standardized access to an existing enterprise information system (EIS) from the JEE platform. Frequently, but not necessarily, these EISs are mainframe systems (green screen scraping and so on). A complete JCA system will have three main components: the EIS itself, the resource adaptor that implements the connector specification, and the Java EE-compliant application server, which uses the resource adaptor to access the EIS. The JCA focuses on the non-functional characteristics you would expect for a part of the JEE platform targeted squarely at large, established systems—for example, full support for transaction context propagation to preserve Atomicity, Consistency, Isolation, and Durability (ACID) semantics across application boundaries, scalability, and correct recovery from failed/interrupted operations.

Essential Points

- The Java EE 5 platform supports multiple methods to support application integration and messaging, both between Java-based systems and between Java and non-Java systems. The choice of which mechanism to use should always be driven by the business requirements and existing architecture.

- We have proposed a set of questions that when answered, should point toward the most appropriate solution to any given scenario. Key requirements to identify and take into account are synchronous vs. asynchronous, security, transactions, guaranteed delivery, the nature of the sending and receiving system and the need for interoperability. Put together, these topics provide you with a general framework to select the right approach for a given integration scenario every time.

- The Java EE 5 platform provides comprehensive support for web services, through multiple specifications. Of these specifications, JAX-WS 2.0, along with JAXB, is the most important to revise.

- The core asynchronous messaging technology used in the JEE 5 platform between Java systems is JMS, or the Java Message Service.

- The Java Connector Architecture, or JCA, is used to integrate the JEE 5 platform with Enterprise Information Systems (EISs). These are typically mainframe-based, legacy systems that need to be exposed via a resource adaptor as a service that can be invoked by code running within a Java EE application server.

Review Your Progress

These questions test your level of accomplishment in analyzing the integration requirements for a given scenario:

1. You have been asked to recommend an asynchronous integration mechanism between two systems, A and B, both written in Java. What do you recommend?

A. Web services

B. Java Connector Architecture (JCA)

C. JMS

D. Session beans

Answer: C. For the stated problem domain (an asynchronous connector between two Java-based systems), JMS is the only appropriate choice. The other three options are viable mechanisms, but far less efficient options.

2. You have been asked to recommend an integration mechanism for two systems, A and B, but only A is written in Java. What do you recommend?

A. Web services

B. Java Connector Architecture (JCA)

C. JMS

D. Session beans

Answer: A. A logical continuation of the first question, in this question, we remove the fact that both system A and B are Java-based. We also remove the fact that an asynchronous connector is required. This removes JMS. Answer B is not warranted because neither system is an Enterprise Information Source (EIS). Answer D does not address the non-Java component. Because of the interoperability features of web services, Answer A is the correct option.

3. What are two web service support features in Java EE? (Select all that apply.)

A. Generating a web service from an entity class

B. Generating a Java class from a WSDL file

C. Generating a web service from a stateful session bean

D. Associating a JMS queue with a WSDL file

E. Generating a web service from a stateless session bean

Answers: B and E. Answer A is not possible, nor is answer C—only stateless session beans can act as web service end point implementations. Answer D attempts to combine two concepts that make no sense: a delivery mechanism for asynchronous

Java, and Java messaging with a descriptor for a web service. Answers B and E are core elements of the JEE support for web services.

4. Merchant bank XYZ has an existing Enterprise Information Source (EIS) that is to be used on a new online banking project. You have been tasked with recommending how this should be achieved. (Select the most appropriate solution.)

   A. Expose the EIS using JSPs, Servlets, and EJBs.
   B. Expose the EIS as a JCA-compliant resource adaptor.
   C. Expose the EIS as an entity bean using JPA.
   D. Expose the EIS using JMS.

   Answer: B. When it's an EIS that needs integrating, JCA is always top of the list. The other answers could be made to work eventually, but are clearly sub-optimal when compared to B.

5. ABC is a commodity marketplace, accepting millions of bids on items from wheat to pork bellies every day. Bids are queued and processed offline. You have been asked to recommend the interface to use between the Java application server that hosts the presentation tier and the Java application server that hosts the marketplace itself. What do you recommend?

   A. A Java Connector Architecture-compliant resource adaptor
   B. A JMS queue with message-driven beans to process incoming messages
   C. Entity beans built using JPA
   D. A web service

   Answer: B. The cues in the question to select B are the Java-to-Java nature of the integration and the fact that bids are not processed immediately. They are processed offline (that is, asynchronously), which is a key indicator that a JMS solution is the right answer. None of the other answers—A, C, and D—meet the dual requirements of asynchronousity and Java–Java integration.

6. ACME Corporation has just acquired ABC Corp—its biggest competitor. ACME uses Java technology extensively, while ABC Corp uses the Microsoft .NET platform. You have been tasked with recommending an interim integration solution that will allow ACME to leverage ABC resources from the outset, while minimizing the time, cost, and risk of doing this. What do you recommend?

   A. A JMS queue, with MDBs consuming messages sent from ABC Corp systems
   B. A JCA-compliant resource adaptor between ACME and ABC
   C. A web services layer between ACME and ABC
   D. Re-implement ABC's business logic using JSF, stateless session beans, and JPA

   Answer: D. Given the business problem description, web services is the most appropriate manner to integrate code written on the .NET platform into ACME's systems, while minimizing time, cost, and risk to the company. Answer A is not appropriate given the heterogeneous nature of ACME and ABC systems, B is not appropriate because ABC's systems are not legacy, and D, although potentially a longer-term solution or roadmap, does not minimize time, cost, or risk.

7. From the following list, select the most relevant characteristics of a service-oriented architecture (SOA)-based system. (Select all that apply.)

   A. Entity classes performance
   B. Loose coupling
   C. XML web services
   D. Stateful session handling in a load-balanced cluster
   E. Well-defined contracts between message producers and consumers

   Answers: B and E. Answer A is a red herring, as are answers C and D. Although all are valid concerns, none of these options will be directly improved or degraded through the adoption of SOA. However, answers B and E are directly impacted by the adoption of SOA in a system architecture.

8. ACME bank is launching a new SMS notification service to notify (informational messages only) customers via their mobile phones of transactions and account changes. ACME bank operates world-wide and has over 500 million named customers, and expected message volumes are high. What is the most scalable way for ACME bank to send messages to the mobile device notification channel for onward transmission as SMS text messages? (Select the best answer.)

A. Guaranteed messaging using message-driven beans (MDBs) consuming messages from a JMS queue populated by the systems of record

B. Web services retrieving records of interest directly from the core systems

C. Unguaranteed messaging using message-driven beans (MDBs) consuming messages from a JMS queue populated by the systems of record

D. Stateless session beans retrieving records of interest directly from the core systems using XML messaging

Answer: C. Answers B and D tightly couple the systems together, reducing scalability. Answer A requires guaranteed messaging when the messages are informational only. Answer C fulfills the business requirements in the best and most complete fashion.

CHAPTER 6

Security

- Explain the client-side security model for the Java SE environment, including the Web Start and applet deployment modes.
- Given an architectural system specification, select appropriate locations for implementation of specified security features, and select suitable technologies for implementation of those features.
- Identify and classify potential threats to a system and describe how a given architecture will address the threats.
- Describe the commonly used declarative and programmatic methods used to secure applications built on the Java EE platform—for example, use of deployment descriptors and JAAS.

Introduction

Security is quite possibly the most overlooked aspect of many JEE-based systems, yet failure to ensure that a system is properly secured possesses the most potential to inflict serious damage to the underlying business. As a JEE architect, you must understand the Java security model not just on the server, but on the client as well—thus the inclusion of the first item in the previous objectives list for this section. The primary security-related objectives of any JEE system are as follows:

- **Confidentiality**—Ensure that the system data and functions are protected from unauthorized access.
- **Integrity**—Ensure (provably) that system data has not been modified or interfered with by a third party (malicious or not).
- **Authentication**—Ensure that the identity of a user or a remote system accessing the system is valid and correct and has not been impersonated or compromised in any way.

- **Authorization**—Ensure that a valid, authenticated user or remote system has the appropriate rights to access system data or execute system functions.
- **Non-Repudiation**—Ensure that all actions, once performed, cannot be denied by the user or the system itself.

Depending on the industry setting, the use cases you have to solve, and the nature of the business itself, the importance attached to each of these characteristics varies. (For example, anyone can visit www.google. com and execute a search; far fewer people can access a search engine for classified military matters run by a defense company.) In this chapter, we address security as it is addressed by the JEE platform, honing in where appropriate on topics that we believe are especially relevant to the exam situation.

Prerequisite Review

You must be familiar with the following topics and resources relating to security listed here. You are not required to know all of the material here by rote or memorization, but equally, you cannot claim to be a proficient architect unless you understand clearly the underpinnings of the Java security model and how it is then extended and leveraged in higher architecture tiers in the JEE environment. The relevant topics and specifications (with relevant Java Specification Request, or JSR, numbers) are as follows:

- The Java Language Specification (JLS), version 3.0.
- The JAAS API: http://java.sun.com/j2se/1.5.0/docs/guide/ security/jaas/JAASRefGuide.html (Note: The official link is http://java.sun.com/products/jaas, but this link simply redirects to the Java SE Security home page.)
- The WS-Security home page (purely for background reading): http://www.oasis-open.org/committees/tc_home.php?wg_ abbrev=wss#technical.
- Chapter 3 of the Java EE 5 specification.

We examine the seminal aspects and use cases of security in more detail. First, we run through some of the most important security-related concepts in the JEE.

JRE

The sandbox of the Java Runtime Environment (JRE) is a fundamental property of the Java runtime environment and is the basis for all other security layers in the Java programming model. Simply put, the designers of the Java programming language and runtime gave careful consideration to security at design time as well as implementation time, and this has provided higher-level security APIs and abstractions a firm foundation to build on. Basics provided by the JRE/Java programming language include: automatic memory management, strong typing, bytecode verification, and secure class loading. For exam purposes, take all of this as a given, and focus your revision and study efforts on the security APIs and capabilities built on top of these basic capabilities in the JEE platform, including the difference between sandboxed applets and regular Java applications.

JAAS

JAAS, or the Java Authentication and Authorization Service, is the general mechanism supplied by the Java Virtual Machine (JVM), allowing Java code to identify users and roles before allowing or denying access to resources or functionality controlled by the JVM. JAAS was originally a modular install for the JVM but is now built into the JVM and is required by the JEE 5 specification. JAAS supports pluggable authentication and authorization modules, making it possible for architects to integrate existing security services into JAAS. Moreover, the standard JAAS implementation ships with connectors that implement authentication protocols—for example, the Kerberos module.

Credential

A **credential** is a container of information used to authenticate a principal (discussed next) to the System under Development (SuD). Credentials vary significantly depending on the authentication protocol or system used (that is, they are mechanism specific). However, the core purpose is the same—a credential is a structured set of information that an authentication module uses to either allow or deny access to the SuD.

Principal

A **principal** is an entity (a person or system that can be uniquely identified) that can be authenticated by a JEE security module before SuD system access is allowed or denied.

Authentication

Authentication is the process by which the SuD examines the credentials of a named principal in order to recognize that principal as a named user of the SuD. An end user can authenticate to a JEE application using either a web client (that is, a JSP/JSF presentation tier), or an application client (a client-side Java application or applet). The JEE 5 platform requires that all application servers support three specific authentication methods: HTTP basic authentication, SSL mutual authentication, and form-based login.

Authorization

Authorization is the process by which a named principal (who is already authenticated to the SuD) is allowed or disallowed access to a protected SuD named resource based on the permissions granted either directly to them or indirectly through group or role membership. The JEE security model employs a role-based access control mechanism that abstract principals from permissions by the introduction of roles. A principal may belong to one or more roles, and those roles may have zero or more permissions assigned to them.

Discussion

Security is the perennial hot topic in the enterprise application space. Often overlooked in development and under-tested in QA, the security aspects of all applications, including JEE applications, undergo greater scrutiny as corporations of all shapes and sizes realize their potential exposure if data is compromised. Despite its unwieldiness in some scenarios, the JEE platform has robust support for ensuring that a JEE application can do the following:

- Control access to application data as necessary with fine granularity
- Control access to application business logic as necessary with fine granularity
- Encrypt and decrypt data as necessary to provide secure messaging
- Co-operate with existing enterprise resource systems (ERSs) to control access to data and business logic contained within those ERSs as necessary

These capabilities are not accidental. From its inception, the JEE platform has been designed and enhanced to meet the needs of applications that need a strong and comprehensive security model end to end. We now consider the most important features of the JEE platform.

Client-Side Security

In this section, we need to consider applets run by the browser via the Java plug-in and applications deployed via Java Web Start or installed directly on the machine.

Both Web Start applications and applets run inside a sandbox environment, which allows the end user to control what client-side resources the code can and cannot access or modify. Compiled Java bytecode must be signed before it can request access to these resources—all code attempting to access client-side resources, such as the local file system, or to open a socket to another server will prompt the end user with a modal dialog to permit or deny the operation.

Java applications installed directly onto a client machine do not run inside a sandbox, and no permissions are checked before an operation is executed.

Regardless of how an application has been deployed to a remote machine, once there the architect's job is to ensure that sensitive data passed between the server and the client is encrypted and impenetrable to malicious entities. The easiest way to achieve this is to encrypt all data using Secure Sockets Layer (SSL). Java supports this both to encrypt RMI traffic (RMI over SSL) and to encrypt HTTP traffic (HTTP over SSL, or HTTPS).

Server-Side Security

Here we need to consider the EJB and web containers, JMS, and access to Enterprise Information Stores (EISs), which are discussed next.

EJB Container

The EJB container provides two methods on the `EJBContext` interface to allow developers to programmatically check a user's permission before invoking a method containing potentially sensitive business logic. These methods are as follows:

- `isCallerInRole`
- `getCallerPrincipal`

Looking beyond these methods, developers also control code running in the EJB container using declarations—specifying at design time what users and roles can access specific EJB methods. The method-permission element contains a list of methods that can be accessed by a named role. Finally, the EJB container enables the developer to define a "run as" capability, whereby the original identity of the caller is substituted in favor of an identity defined declaratively.

Web Container

Like the EJB container, Servlets and JSPs running in the web container also have access to security information at runtime to decide whether to allow or deny access to incoming requests. These methods are part of the `HttpServletRequest` interface and are as follows:

- `isUserInRole`
- `getUserPrincipal`

From a security perspective, the web container typically has to do more work than the EJB container as it is the external face of the application. Many JEE applications are designed around the premise that the web layer does most, if not all, of the security work (authentication and authorization). If a request makes it through the web layer, many systems allow that request unquestioned access to the SuD resources. The primary mechanism used to allow or deny a named user access to SuD functionality is simply to use URL authorization. In this mechanism, the URLs of the application are defined to have a specific security meaning that can be ascertained using regular expressions—for example, "all URLs of the form /admin/* should only be accessible to users that have been assigned the Administrator role." At design time, these rules are captured in the web.xml for the web application, and the web server uses these rules at runtime to enforce access—that is, the web server's security policy is derived from the deployment descriptor.

We can capture the sequence of events that occur when a user attempts to access a secured resource via a URL, as follows:

- On the first attempt to access a secured resource, the user is redirected to a login page by the web server, which detects that the user in question has not been authenticated or authorized.
- The user fills in a form that collects the required authentication data (usually a username and password, but this can vary).
- This form is posted back to the web server where the user is validated by the web server.
- The web server sets a credential for the user for the duration of the session to determine what resources can and cannot be accessed or invoked by the user in question.

Figure 6-1 depicts the sequence of steps in diagrammatic form.

Putting the EJB Container and Web Container Together

The EJB container and web container maintain separate security contexts, each derived at runtime from information contained in the EJB and web deployment descriptors. Therefore, when a web resource (for example, a JSP page) attempts to invoke an EJB resource to complete a business action, the EJB container first uses the security context/credential associated with the JSP call to authorize (or reject) the request. If the request is authorized, the web container passes control of the request to the EJB container and, when completed, the result of the operation is returned to the web container for further processing, and ultimately to be displayed to the end user.

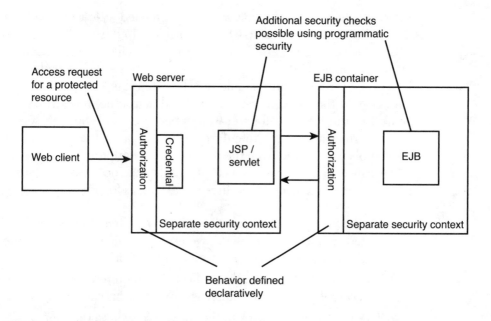

Figure 6-1   The set of steps involved in authenticating and authorizing access to a controlled resource by a JEE web server.

Web Service Security

The standardization of all aspects of web services is a moving feast, because of its main use case—to allow heterogeneous systems to inter-operate. The security aspects of web services are no different. Web services security is defined in the WS-Security standards controlled by OASIS. Broadly speaking, WS-Security addresses the topic of web services security as follows:

- **Authentication and authorization**—Using credentials.
- **Message-level data integrity**—Using XML signatures.
- **Message-level and transport confidentiality**—Using encryption.

As far as the JEE 5 platform goes, support for web services security is not as complete as desired, and it is likely that this aspect of the platform will be tightened up in the JEE 6 release, via initiatives such as Project

Metro (https://metro.dev.java.net/) and the XML and Web Services Security Project XWSS (https://xwss.dev.java.net/).

As far as this discussion goes, we simply relate what is set in stone in section 11.3.2 of JSR 224 (the JSR describing JAX-WS; see Chapter 5, "Integration and Messaging," for more details on JAX-WS), namely that all JEE 5-compliant servers with an implementation of the XML/HTTP binding must support HTTP basic authentication using two properties to configure authentication information (`javax.xml.ws.security. auth.username` and `javax.xml.ws.security.auth.password`).

In addition to this authentication support, transport-level encryption is also supported. However, message-level encryption is not supported or required in a standard implementation, although multiple mechanisms do exist to support message-level encryption if required.

How Security Behavior Is Defined

In this section, we examine how the JEE application serves is instructed on how to enforce a desired security policy for a JEE application. In short, there are two distinct ways for a programmer/application assembler to express how an application should perform security tasks, such as user authentication and authorization, declaratively and programmatically. We now examine each in turn.

Declarative Security

In the declarative security model, the JVM is instructed on the valid users and roles for the system under consideration via a well-formed XML file (the deployment descriptor) and the specific resources and operations that those users and roles can access and execute in the JVM. This method of security definition is especially pervasive in the JEE environment, and is implemented in the EJB and Servlet containers. The programmer or architect expresses his or her intent with regard to security by providing details on security roles, access control, and authentication requirements in the deployment descriptor, which is then transformed by the container at run-time into its internal representation or security policy dictating how to govern the application's security. This method has a number of advantages over programmatic security:

- The security configuration is obvious, self-evident, and contained in one place.

- The security configuration can be modified at deployment time without needing to recompile source code, making the application more configurable.

Finally, a new addition to the JEE 5 platform is the addition of annotations, in sympathy with the overall design intent of striving to make the JEE 5 platform as easy to program as possible. Instead of needing to compose a large and often-complex EJB or web deployment descriptor, the programmer can simply use annotations such as `javax.annotation.security.RolesAllowed` to instruct the relevant container directly in the source code. This is not the same as programmatic security (discussed next), where the programmer calls specific methods in order to decide how to service a business request; annotations are a more programmer-friendly way of defining security in a declarative fashion. If desired, the application assembler can choose to override the values embedded in the source code of the application at deployment time if the default values do not suffice for the intended use.

Programmatic Security

In addition to or instead of declarative security, the JVM can also execute security checks that are not defined in an external deployment descriptor, but defined in the running code itself. Programmatic security refers to security intents expressed directly within the code of a JEE application—that is, not externalized to a separate dedicated section of the deployment descriptor. The four methods listed next allow server-side components to service incoming requests taking into account the identity (including role and permissions) of the caller. In practice, most applications use a combination of both declarative and programmatic security checks to provide a higher level of security than either approach alone. The key methods to be aware of that provide access to security information are the following:

- `isCallerInRole` (EJBContext)
- `getCallerPrincipal` (EJBContext)
- `isUserInRole` (HttpServletRequest)
- `getUserPrincipal` (HttpServletRequest)

Commonly Encountered Security Threats

In this section, we touch on the most commonly encountered security threats and how they are typically addressed in JEE applications. No security threat list can ever be truly exhaustive or up to date, however, and the reader is encouraged to augment this section with online research. Here are some of these security threats:

- **Man in the middle attacks**—An attack where the malicious party intercepts messages sent between the client and server as part of a valid conversation or transaction, either to gain access to unauthorized information or to achieve an outcome favorable to the malicious party. Encrypting all network traffic using strong SSL guards effectively against this attack.

- **Session hijacking (replaying data)**—An attack related to man in the middle where the malicious party inspects the SuD and identifies how the server recognizes connected clients. The malicious party then steals the identity of a real client and uses that to interact with the server—again, typically either to gain unauthorized access to data or to achieve an outcome desirable to the malicious party and undesirable to the trusted party. Strong data encryption helps here, but architects must also ensure that no sensitive information is used in the application URL that would help a hacker to hijack a session.

- **Password cracking**—An attack where brute force is used to repeatedly attempt to login as a valid user by guessing their password. This attack can be easily countered using business logic that places minimum complexity rules on passwords selected by users and also shuts the user out of the system if more than a specified number of login attempts fail.

- **Phishing**—An attack where users are misdirected to a false or hoax version of the SuD and tricked into releasing sensitive information. The valid information is then used by the malicious party to gain access to the SuD. Phishing is as much about educating users as it is an engineering problem, but server-side approaches include monitoring for unusual SuD activity on the part of users.

- **Social hacking**—An attack where social engineering often involving members of the opposite sex are used to gain unauthorized access to the SuD. At the time of writing, no Java API or library existed to counter this insidious, yet exciting, attack vector.

- **Network sniffing**—One of the simplest and oldest attacks; unencrypted data is simply read from the network using a sniffing tool. Typically, man in the middle, session hijack attacks, and so on are built on top of a sniffing attack. Strong data encryption is an effective and easy response to this threat.

- **For web applications that use JavaScript or XSS (cross-site scripting, Type 0, 1, and 2) attacks**—In general, the advent of rich internet applications (RIAs) introduce security risks that a JEE architect must be aware of and resolve.

Defining a Security Model

The scope of security is wide-ranging, with serious implications if any compromise occurs. Therefore, the JEE architect is well advised to create and maintain a security model—effectively, a roadmap or blueprint that explains how their JEE application enforces security, across all of the topics and threats covered in this chapter. The model itself will not guarantee a secure application, but it will serve to ensure that the architect considers the threats faced and the measures employed to counteract them. At a minimum, the model should cover the following:

- Underlying system infrastructure (hardware, including the networking layer and components)
- User authentication
- User authorization
- Auditing
- Data encryption
- System hardening against specific attacks, as detailed in the previous "Commonly Encountered Security Threats" section

Essential Points

- Security is a cross-cutting concern across all layers of a JEE application—from the client to the persistence tier.
- JEE's approach to security is robust. The underlying Java platform possesses basic capabilities that eliminate memory buffer attacks and so on. JEE augments that capability with the tools that allow a JEE architect to both programmatically and declaratively define who should have access and to what in the SuD.

Review Your Progress

These questions test your level of accomplishment in analyzing the integration requirements for a given scenario:

1. You are the architect for a social networking application that allows users to leave comments for other users. Recently, a spate of hacker attacks have disrupted the site, reducing revenue from site partners and advertising. Of the attack types listed next, which two can be addressed by ensuring that all special characters/word sequences are removed from all free text inputs on the web site?

   A. Buffer overflow
   B. Cross-site scripting
   C. SQL injection
   D. Permission errors

   Answers: C and D. Patrolling and validating the free text elements of a web application is directly relevant and essential to ensuring that XSS attacks and malicious SQL commands cannot be executed. Answer A is a misnomer, as is D.

2. Which two checks are made possible in the byte-code verification?

    A. Memory usage is controlled.

    B. Access to some files is checked.

    C. Digital signatures are verified.

    D. Data type conversions are checked/controlled.

    E. The language access restrictions (for example, private or protected) are respected.

    Answers: C and E. A, D, and B are not checked by the process of byte code verification, as evidenced by the fact that Java applications can run out of memory, access to a given file can be denied at runtime, and casting exceptions can also occur at runtime.

3. You are architecting a DVD rental application that accepts customer feedback. Users can rank movies from one to five by clicking on buttons, as well as input comments about the movie into a text box. Which two can be addressed by filtering special characters from text boxes on JSP forms? (Select all that apply.)

    A. SQL injection

    B. Buffer overflow

    C. Authorization errors

    D. Cross-site scripting

    E. Rootkit attacks

    Answers: A and D. Answer B cannot occur in a Java runtime environment, whereas C and E are general security issues, and not directly related to the issue of validating free text entry by end users (malicious or otherwise).

4. The web pages in a system are carefully designed so that links to security-sensitive URLs are not available in pages offered to untrusted users. Which statement is true? (Select the best answer.)

    A. The system security is adequately protected by this approach.

    B. Every security-sensitive target must be additionally protected using the declarative security model.

C. The system security is adequately protected by this approach, provided only POST requests are accepted by the server.

D. The system security is adequately protected by this approach, provided only GET requests are accepted by the server.

Answer: B. Answers A, C, and D all represent a lax or incomplete attitude toward the risk of an untrusted user using basic techniques to identify the fully qualified names of the security-sensitive URLs. Only choosing to use the declarative security model (answer B), which forces authentication and authorization, is a true reflection of the security needed.

5. Security restrictions in a use-case require that the behavior of an EJB business method vary according to the role of the user. How should this be achieved? (Select the best answer.)

A. The deployment descriptor is written using the roles determined by the programmer.

B. The programmer determines a role reference and uses it in the code. This is mapped to a role in the deployment descriptor.

C. The business method determines the role of the user using JNDI and configuration information in the deployment descriptor.

D. The business method determines the role of the user using JAAS and configuration information in the deployment descriptor.

Answer: D. Answer D uses the JAAS framework in the manner in which it was intended—to ascertain at runtime the role of the current principal and to match it to the roles authorized to execute the EJB method in question. Answers A and B do not address how the runtime check takes place. Answer C selects JNDI (Java Naming and Directory Interface) when JAAS is the security framework.

6. A malicious hacker is trying to crash your web site by using various denial of service attacks. Which two flaws should you protect against for this specific threat?

   A. XSS attacks
   B. Authentication failures
   C. Man in the middle attacks
   D. Session hijacking
   E. Weak password exploits
   F. Authorization failures

   Answers: C and D. Answers A and E, although both are security issues, are not related directly to DoS attacks. B and F are normal occurrences in an application lifecycle (although they should be logged to identify attempts to gain unauthorized access to the SuD). C and D are well-known mechanisms through which to launch DoS attacks on a system.

CHAPTER 7

Applying Patterns

- From a list, select the most appropriate pattern for a given scenario. Patterns are limited to those documented in this book—*Core J2EE Patterns: Best Practices and Design Strategies*, 2nd Edition; Alur, Crupi, and Malks (2003 Edition)—and named using the names given in that book.

- From a list, select the most appropriate pattern for a given scenario. Patterns are limited to those documented in this book—*Design Patterns: Elements of Reusable Object-Oriented Software*; Gamma, Erich, Richard Helm, Ralph Johnson, and John Vlissides (1995 Edition)—and are named using the names given in that book.

- Select from a list the benefits and drawbacks of a pattern drawn from the book—*Design Patterns: Elements of Reusable Object-Oriented Software*; Gamma, Erich, Richard Helm, Ralph Johnson, and John Vlissides (1995 Edition).

- Select from a list the benefits and drawbacks of a specified Core J2EE pattern drawn from the book—*Core J2EE Patterns: Best Practices and Design Strategies*, 2nd Edition; Alur, Crupi, and Malks (2003 Edition).

Introduction

Christopher Alexander, a building architect, introduced the notion of patterns in the 1970s. He realized that there were certain solutions that you could apply over and over again to the same or similar problems. He also combined these existing solutions to create new solutions to a new problem. In 1987, Ward Cunningham and Kent Beck developed five patterns to use in interface design. But it wasn't until 1994 that Erich Gamma, Richard Helm, John Vlissides, and Ralph Johnson published the now-famous book *Design Patterns: Elements of Reusable Object-Oriented Software*, which described a way of documenting patterns that has become the industry standard. These men are often referred to as the Gang of Four (GoF).

In 1999, Sun Microsystems introduced Java2 Enterprise Edition. The Sun Java Center, the Java consulting practice in Sun Professional Services, noticed that companies were not using the technology correctly and architecting solutions that would not scale. John Crupi, Deepak Alur, and Danny Malks embarked on a mission to document the appropriate patterns to successfully architect a J2EE solution correctly—thus, *Core J2EE Patterns: Best Practices and Design Strategies* was created.

This chapter describes how you can use patterns to help you create an architecture. These patterns are usually at the object and class level, but they can also be abstracted to a higher level.

Prerequisite Review

This chapter will focus on the Gang of Four (GoF) patterns, as described in *Design Patterns: Elements of Reusable Object-Oriented Software* and Core J2EE patterns, as described in *Core J2EE Patterns*, Crupi, et al. The following assumptions about your knowledge of patterns will be applied to this chapter:

- Able to describe each of the Gang of Four design patterns
- Able to describe each of the Core J2EE patterns
- Categorize a pattern as either Core J2EE pattern or GoF design pattern based on the name
- Understand the basics of applying patterns

Discussion

The GoF patterns are categorized into three categories, as follows:

- **Creational**—Support the creation of objects
- **Structural**—Deal with relationships between portions of your application
- **Behavioral**—Influence how state and behavior flow through the system

Creational Patterns

Creational patterns support the creation of objects in a system. Creational patterns allow objects to be created in a system without having to identify a specific class type in the code, so you do not have to write large, complex code to instantiate an object. It does this by having the subclass of the class create the objects. However, this can limit the type or number of objects that can be created within a system. The Creational patterns are Abstract Factory, Builder, Factory Method, Prototype, and Singleton.

Abstract Factory Pattern

This pattern provides an interface for creating families of related or dependent objects without specifying their concrete classes.

Given a set of related abstract classes, the Abstract Factory pattern provides a way to create instances of those abstract classes from a matched set of concrete subclasses. Figure 7-1 illustrates the Abstract Factory pattern.

The Abstract Factory pattern provides an abstract class that determines the appropriate concrete class to instantiate to create a set of concrete products that implement a standard interface. The client interacts only with the product interfaces and the Abstract Factory class. The client never knows about the concrete construction classes provided by this pattern.

The Abstract Factory pattern is similar to the Factory Method pattern, except it creates families of related objects.

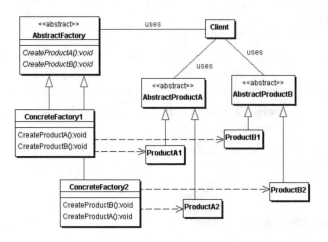

Figure 7-1   Abstract Factory pattern diagram

Benefits

The following lists the benefits of using the Abstract Factory pattern:

- Isolates the concrete classes from client
- Allows for exchanging product families easy
- Promotes consistency among products by implementing the common interface

When to Use

You should use the Abstract Factory pattern when:

- The system should be independent of how its products are created, composed, and represented.
- The system should be configured with one of multiple families of products—for example, Microsoft Windows or Apple OSX classes.
- The family of related product objects is designed to be used together, and you must enforce this constraint. This is the key point of the pattern; otherwise, you could use a Factory Method.
- You want to provide a class library of products, and reveal only their interfaces, not their implementations.

Builder Pattern

The Builder pattern separates the construction of a complex object from its representation so the same construction process can create different objects. The Builder pattern allows a client object to construct a complex object by specifying only its type and content. The client is shielded from the details of the object's construction. This simplifies the creation of complex objects by defining a class that builds instances of another class. The Builder pattern produces one main product, and there might be more than one class in the product, but there is always one main class. Figure 7-2 illustrates the Builder pattern.

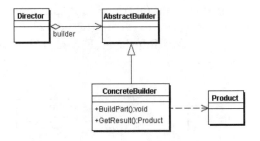

Figure 7-2   Builder pattern diagram

When you use the Builder pattern, you create the complex objects one step at a time. Other patterns build the object in a single step.

Benefits

The following lists the benefits of using the Builder pattern:

■ Lets you vary a product's internal representation

■ Isolates code for construction and representation

■ Gives you greater control over the construction process

When to Use

You should use the Builder pattern when

■ The algorithm for creating a complex object should be independent of both the parts that make up the object and how these parts are assembled.

■ The construction process must allow different representations of the constructed object.

Factory Method Pattern

The Factory Method pattern defines an interface for creating an object, but lets the subclasses decide which class to instantiate. The Factory Method lets a class defer instantiation to subclasses, which is useful for constructing individual objects for a specific purpose without the requestor knowing the specific class being instantiated. This enables you to introduce new classes without modifying the code because the new class implements only the interface so it can be used by the client. You create a new factory class to create the new class, and the factory class implements the factory interface. Figure 7-3 illustrates the Factory Method pattern.

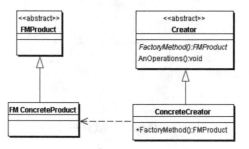

Figure 7-3   Factory Method pattern diagram

Benefits

The following lists the benefits of using the Factory Method pattern:

■ Eliminates the need to bind application classes into your code. The code deals only with the interface, so you can work with any classes that implement that interface.

■ Enables the subclasses to provide an extended version of an object, because creating an object inside a class is more flexible than creating the object directly in the client.

When to Use

You should use the Factory Method pattern when:

- A class cannot anticipate the class of objects it must create.
- A class wants its subclasses to specify the objects it creates.
- Classes delegate responsibility to one of several helper subclasses, and you want to localize the knowledge of which helper subclass is the delegate.

Prototype Pattern

The Prototype pattern allows an object to create customized objects without knowing their exact class or the details of how to create them. It specifies the kinds of objects to create using a prototypical instance and creates new objects by copying this prototype. The Prototype pattern works by giving prototypical objects to an object and then initiates the creation of objects. The creation-initiating object then creates objects by asking the prototypical objects to make copies of themselves. The Prototype pattern makes creating objects dynamically easier by defining classes whose objects can duplicate themselves. Figure 7-4 illustrates the Prototype pattern.

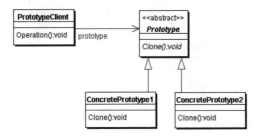

Figure 7-4   Prototype pattern diagram

Benefits

The following lists the benefits of using the Prototype pattern:

- Adding and removing products at run time
- Specifying new objects by varying values

- Specifying new objects by varying structure
- Reducing subclasses
- Configuring an application with classes dynamically

When to Use

You should use the Prototype pattern when:

- The classes to instantiate are specified at run time—for example, by dynamic loading
- To avoid building a class hierarchy of factories that parallels the class hierarchy of products
- When instances of a class can have one of only a few different combinations of state

Singleton Pattern

The Singleton pattern ensures that a class has only one instance and provides a global point of access to that class. It ensures that all objects that use an instance of this class use the same instance. Figure 7-5 illustrates the Singleton pattern.

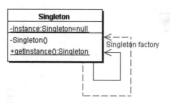

Figure 7-5   Singleton pattern diagram

Benefits

The following lists the benefits of using the Singleton pattern:

- Controlled access to sole instance
- Reduced name space
- Permits refinement of operations and representation

- Permits a variable number of instances
- More flexible than class operations

When to Use

You should use the Singleton pattern when:

- There must be exactly one instance of a class.

Structural Patterns

Structural patterns control the relationships between large portions of your applications. Structural patterns affect applications in a variety of ways—for example, the Adapter pattern enables two incompatible systems to communicate, whereas the Façade pattern enables you to present a simplified interface to a user without removing all the options available in the system.

Structural patterns enable you to create systems without rewriting or customizing the code. This provides the system with enhanced reusability and robust functionality.

The structural patterns are Adapter, Bridge, Composite, Decorator, Façade, Flyweight, and Proxy.

Adapter Pattern

The Adapter pattern acts as an intermediary between two classes, converting the interface of one class so that it can be used with the other. This enables classes with incompatible interfaces to work together. The Adapter pattern implements an interface known to its clients and provides access to an instance of a class not known to its clients. An adapter object provides the functionality of an interface without having to know the class used to implement that interface. Figure 7-6 illustrates the Adapter pattern.

Benefits

The following lists the benefits of using the Adapter pattern:

- Allows two or more incompatible objects to communicate and interact
- Improves reusability of older functionality

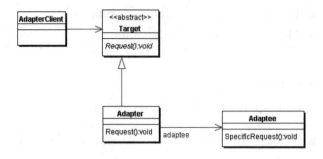

Figure 7-6   Adapter pattern diagram

When to Use

You should use the Adapter pattern when:

- You want to use an existing class, and its interface does not match the interface you need.
- You want to create a reusable class that cooperates with unrelated or unforeseen classes—that is, classes that don't necessarily have compatible interfaces.
- You want to use an object in an environment that expects an interface that is different from the object's interface.
- Interface translation among multiple sources must occur.

Bridge Pattern

The Bridge pattern divides a complex component into two separate but related inheritance hierarchies: the functional abstraction and the internal implementation. This makes it easier to change either aspect of the component so that the two can vary independently.

The Bridge pattern is useful when there is a hierarchy of abstractions and a corresponding hierarchy of implementations. Rather than combining the abstractions and implementations into many distinct classes, the Bridge pattern implements the abstractions and implementations as independent classes that can be combined dynamically. Figure 7-7 illustrates the Bridge pattern.

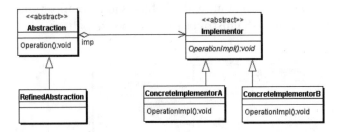

Figure 7-7   Bridge pattern diagram

Benefits

The following lists the benefits of using the Bridge pattern:

- Enables you to separate the interface from the implementation
- Improves extensibility
- Hides implementation details from clients

When to Use

You should use the Bridge pattern when:

- You want to avoid a permanent binding between an abstraction and its implementation.
- Both the abstractions and their implementations should be extensible using subclasses.
- Changes in the implementation of an abstraction should have no impact on clients; that is, you should not have to recompile their code.

Composite Pattern

The Composite pattern enables you to create hierarchical tree structures of varying complexity, while allowing every element in the structure to operate with a uniform interface. The Composite pattern combines objects into tree structures to represent either the whole hierarchy or a part of the hierarchy. This means the Composite pattern

allows clients to treat individual objects and compositions of objects uni-
formly. Figure 7-8 illustrates the Composite pattern.

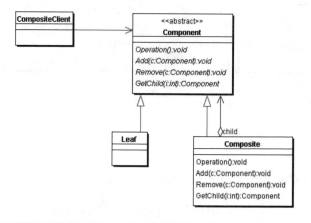

Figure 7-8   Composite pattern diagram

Benefits

The following lists the benefits of using the Composite pattern:

- Defines class hierarchies consisting of primitive objects and com-
  posite objects
- Makes it easier to add new kinds of components
- Provides flexibility of structure and a manageable interface

When to Use

You should use the Composite pattern when:

- You want to represent the whole hierarchy or a part of the hierarchy of objects.
- You want clients to be able to ignore the difference between compositions of objects and individual objects.
- The structure can have any level of complexity and is dynamic.

Decorator Pattern

The Decorator pattern enables you to add or remove object functionality without changing the external appearance or function of the object. It changes the functionality of an object in a way that is transparent to its clients by using an instance of a subclass of the original class that delegates operations to the original object. The Decorator pattern attaches additional responsibilities to an object dynamically to provide a flexible alternative to changing object functionality without using static inheritance. Figure 7-9 shows the decorator pattern.

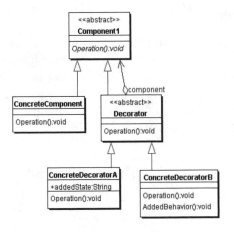

Figure 7-9   Decorator pattern diagram

Benefits

The following lists the benefits of using the Decorator pattern:

- More flexibility than static inheritance
- Avoids feature-laden classes high up in the hierarchy
- Simplifies coding because you write a series of classes, each targeted at a specific part of the functionality, rather than coding all behavior into the object
- Enhances the object's extensibility because you make changes by coding new classes

When to Use

You should use the Decorator pattern when:

- You want to add responsibilities to individual objects dynamically and transparently—that is, without affecting other objects.
- You want to add responsibilities to the object that you might want to change in the future.
- Extension by static subclassing is impractical.

Façade Pattern

The Façade pattern provides a unified interface to a group of interfaces in a subsystem. The Façade pattern defines a higher-level interface that makes the subsystem easier to use because you have only one interface. This unified interface enables an object to access the subsystem using the interface to communicate with the subsystem. Figure 7-10 illustrates the Façade pattern.

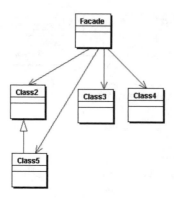

Figure 7-10   Façade pattern diagram

Benefits

The following lists the benefits of using the Façade pattern:

- Provides a simple interface to a complex system without reducing the options provided by the system

- Shields clients from subsystem components
- Promotes weak coupling between the subsystem and its clients
- Reduces coupling between subsystems if every subsystem uses its own Façade pattern and other parts of the system use the Façade pattern to communicate with the subsystem
- Translates the client requests to the subsystems that can fulfill those requests

When to Use

You should use the Façade pattern when:

- You want to provide a simple interface to a complex subsystem.
- There are many dependencies between clients and the implementation classes of an abstraction.
- You want to layer your subsystems.

Flyweight Pattern

The Flyweight pattern reduces the number of low-level, detailed objects within a system by sharing objects. If instances of a class that contain the same information can be used interchangeably, the Flyweight pattern allows a program to avoid the expense of multiple instances that contain the same information by sharing one instance. Figure 7-11 illustrates the Flyweight pattern.

Benefits

The following lists the benefits of using the Flyweight pattern:

- Reduction in the number of objects to handle
- Reduction in memory and on storage devices, if the objects are persisted

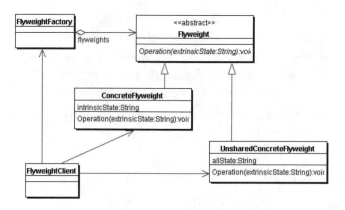

Figure 7-11 Flyweight pattern diagram

When to Use

You should use the Flyweight pattern when all of the following are true:

- The application uses a large number of objects.
- Storage costs are high because of the quantity of objects.
- The application doesn't depend on object identity.

Proxy Pattern

The Proxy pattern provides a surrogate or placeholder object to control access to the original object. There are several types of implementations of the Proxy pattern, with the Remote proxy and Virtual proxy being the most common. Figure 7-12 illustrates the Proxy pattern.

Benefits

The following lists the benefits of using the Proxy pattern:

- A remote proxy can hide the fact that an object resides in a different address space.
- A virtual proxy can perform optimizations, such as creating an object on demand.

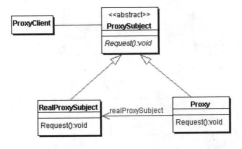

Figure 7-12 Proxy pattern diagram

When to Use

You should use the Proxy pattern when:

- You need a more versatile or sophisticated reference to an object than a simple pointer.

Behavioral Patterns

Behavioral patterns influence how state and behavior flow through a system. By optimizing how state and behavior are transferred and modified, you can simplify, optimize, and increase the maintainability of an application.

The Behavioral patterns are Chain of Responsibility, Command, Interpreter, Iterator, Mediator, Memento, Observer, State, Strategy, Template Method, and Visitor

Chain of Responsibility Pattern

The Chain of Responsibility pattern establishes a chain within a system, so that a message can either be handled at the level where it is first received, or be directed to an object that can handle it. Figure 7-13 illustrates Chain of Responsibility pattern.

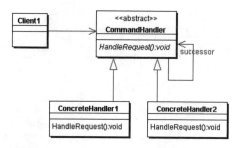

Figure 7-13   Chain of Responsibility pattern diagram

Benefits

The following lists the benefits of using the Chain of Responsibility pattern:

- Reduced coupling
- Added flexibility in assigning responsibilities to objects
- Allows a set of classes to behave as a whole, because events produced in one class can be sent on to other handler classes within the composite

When to Use

You should use the Chain of Responsibility pattern when:

- More than one object can handle a request, and the handler isn't known.
- You want to issue a request to one of several objects without specifying the receiver explicitly.
- The set of objects that can handle a request should be specified dynamically.

Command Pattern

The Command pattern encapsulates a request in an object, which enables you to store the command, pass the command to a method, and return the command like any other object. Figure 7-14 illustrates the Command pattern.

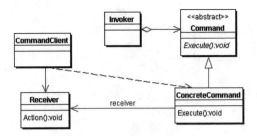

Figure 7-14   Command pattern diagram

Benefits

The following lists the benefits of using the Command pattern:

- It separates the object that invokes the operation from the one that knows how to perform it.
- It's easy to add new commands, because you don't have to change existing classes.

When to Use

You should use the Command pattern when:

- You want to parameterize objects by an action to perform.
- You specify, queue, and execute requests at different times.
- You must support undo, logging, or transactions.

Interpreter Pattern

The Interpreter pattern interprets a language to define a representation for its grammar along with an interpreter that uses the representation to interpret sentences in the language. Figure 7-15 illustrates the Interpreter pattern.

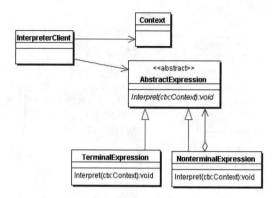

Figure 7-15   Interpreter pattern diagram

Benefits

The following lists the benefits of using the Interpreter pattern:

- It's easy to change and extend the grammar.
- Implementing the grammar is easy.

When to Use

You should use the Interpreter pattern when:

- The grammar of the language is simple.
- Efficiency is not a critical concern.

Iterator Pattern

The Iterator pattern provides a consistent way to sequentially access items in a collection that is independent of and separate from the underlying collection. Figure 7-16 illustrates the Iterator pattern.

Benefits

The following lists the benefits of using the Iterator pattern:

- Supports variations in the traversal of a collection
- Simplifies the interface of the collection

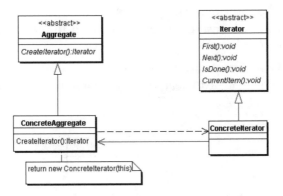

Figure 7-16   Iterator pattern diagram

When to Use

You should use the Iterator pattern to:

- Access collection object's contents without exposing its internal representation
- Support multiple traversals of objects in a collection
- Provide a uniform interface for traversing different structures in a collection

Mediator Pattern

The Mediator pattern simplifies communication among objects in a system by introducing a single object that manages message distribution among other objects. The Mediator pattern promotes loose coupling by keeping objects from referring to each other explicitly, and it lets you vary their interaction independently. Figure 7-17 illustrates the Mediator pattern.

Benefits

The following lists the benefits of using the Mediator pattern:

- Decouples colleagues
- Simplifies object protocols
- Centralizes control

- The individual components become simpler and easier to deal with, because they no longer need to directly pass messages to each other.

- Components are more generic, because they no longer need to contain logic to deal with their communication with other components.

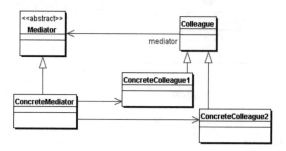

Figure 7-17   Mediator pattern diagram

When to Use

You should use the Mediator pattern when:

- A set of objects communicate in well-defined but complex ways.
- You want to customize a behavior that's distributed between several objects without using subclasses.

Memento Pattern

The Memento pattern preserves a "snapshot" of an object's state, so that the object can return to its original state without having to reveal its content to the rest of the world. Figure 7-18 illustrates the Memento pattern.

Benefits

The following lists the benefits of using the Memento pattern:

- Preserves encapsulation boundaries
- Simplifies the originator

Figure 7-18 Memento pattern diagram

When to Use

You should use the Memento pattern when:

- A snapshot of an object's state must be saved so that it can be restored to that state later.

- Using a direct interface to obtain the state would expose implementation details and break the object's encapsulation.

Observer Pattern

The Observer pattern provides a way for a component to flexibly broadcast messages to interested receivers. It defines a one-to-many dependency between objects so that when one object changes state, all its dependents are notified and updated automatically. Figure 7-19 illustrates the Observer pattern.

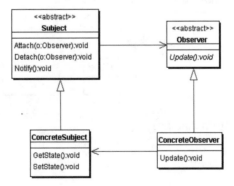

Figure 7-19 Observer pattern diagram

Benefits

The following lists the benefits of using the Observer pattern:

- Abstract coupling between subject and observer
- Support for broadcast communication

When to Use

You should use the Observer pattern when:

- A change to one object requires changing the other object, and you don't know how many objects need to change.
- An object should be able to notify other objects without making assumptions about the identity of those objects.

State Pattern

The State pattern allows an object to alter its behavior when its internal state changes. The object appears to change its class. Figure 7-20 illustrates the State pattern.

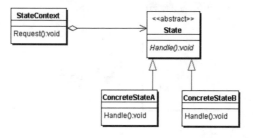

Figure 7-20   State pattern diagram

Benefits

The following lists the benefits of using the State pattern:

- Localizes state-specific behavior and partitions behavior for different states
- Makes state transitions explicit

When to Use

You should use the State pattern when:

- An object's behavior depends on its state, and it must change its behavior at run-time depending on that state.
- Operations have large, multipart conditional statements that depend on the object's state.

Strategy Pattern

The Strategy pattern defines a group of classes that represent a set of possible behaviors. These behaviors can then be used in an application to change its functionality. Figure 7-21 illustrates the Strategy pattern.

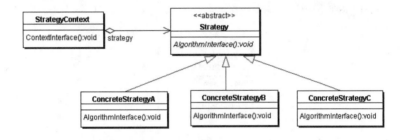

Figure 7-21   Strategy pattern diagram

Benefits

The following lists the benefits of using the Strategy pattern:

- An alternative to subclassing
- Defines each behavior in its own class, which eliminates conditional statements
- Easier to extend a model to incorporate new behaviors without recoding the application

When to Use

You should use the Strategy pattern when:

- Many related classes differ only in their behavior.
- You need different variants of an algorithm.
- An algorithm uses data unknown to clients.

Template Method Pattern

The Template Method pattern provides a method that allows subclasses to override parts of the method without rewriting it. Define the skeleton of an algorithm in an operation, deferring some steps to subclasses. The Template Method lets subclasses redefine certain steps of an algorithm without changing the algorithm's structure. Figure 7-22 illustrates the Template Method pattern.

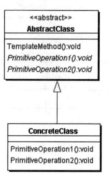

Figure 7-22   Template Method pattern diagram

Benefits

The following is a benefit of using the Template Method pattern:

- Fundamental technique for reusing code

When to Use

You should use the Template Method pattern when:

- You want to implement the invariant parts of an algorithm once and use subclasses to implement the behavior that can vary.
- When common behavior among subclasses should be factored and localized in a common class to avoid code duplication.

Visitor Pattern

The Visitor pattern provides a maintainable, easy way to represent an operation to be performed on the elements of an object structure. The Visitor pattern lets you define a new operation without changing the classes of the elements on which it operates. Figure 7-23 illustrates the Visitor pattern.

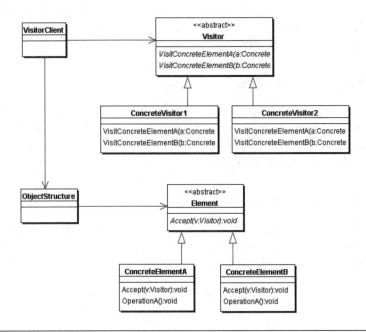

Figure 7-23   Visitor pattern diagram

Benefits

The following lists the benefits of using the Visitor pattern:

- Makes adding new operations easy
- Gathers related operations and separates unrelated ones

When to Use

You should use the Visitor pattern when:

- An object structure contains many classes of objects with differing interfaces, and you want to perform operations on these objects that depend on their concrete classes.
- Classes defining the object structure rarely change, but you often want to define new operations over the structure.

Core Java EE Patterns

The Core J2EE patterns have been very successful in helping organizations architect Java EE systems. A new set of patterns were added when Java EE provided coverage for web services. Some patterns have become obsolete with new technologies introduced in Java EE 5.

Presentation Tier

Presentation tier patterns help organize the components to improve code re-use when presenting data to the client tier. Not all patterns need to be applied in the presentation tier, and some provide the same solution to a common problem.

Intercepting Filter

The Intercepting Filter pattern provides the ability to manipulate a request prior to processing or to manipulate the response before sending the results of the request. Figure 7-24 illustrates the Intercepting Filter pattern.

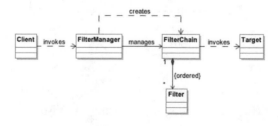

Figure 7-24   Intercepting Filter pattern diagram

Benefits

The following lists the benefits of using the Intercepting Filter pattern:

- Centralizes pre-processing of requests
- Centralizes post-processing of responses

When to Use

You should use the Intercepting Filter pattern when:

- You need to pre-process a request or response.
- You need to post-process a request or response.

Context Object

The Context Object pattern is used to encapsulate the specifics of protocol implementation to be shared. Figure 7-25 illustrates the Context Object pattern.

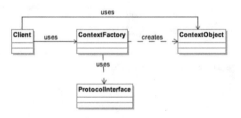

Figure 7-25   Context Object pattern diagram

Benefits

The following lists the benefits of using the Context Object pattern:

- Improves reusability and maintainability
- Allows code to be portable across operating systems

When to Use

You should use the Context Object pattern when:

- Components need access to system information
- Decouple application from underlining protocols and system interfaces

Front Controller

The Front Controller pattern creates central control logic for presentation request handling. The Front Controller is different from the Intercepting Filter in that the Front Controller is determining processing based on the request and an Intercepting Filter is modifying the request. Figure 7-26 illustrates the Front Controller pattern.

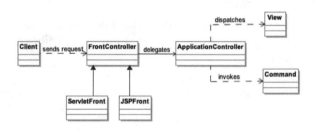

Figure 7-26   Front Controller pattern diagram

Benefits

The following lists the benefits of using the Front Controller pattern:

- Centralizes control logic
- Improves reusability
- Improves separation of concerns

When to Use

You should use the Front Controller pattern to:

- Apply common logic to multiple requests
- Separate processing logic from view

Application Controller

The Application Controller pattern is used to centralize retrieval and invocation of request-processing components, such as commands and views. Figure 7-27 illustrates the Application Controller.

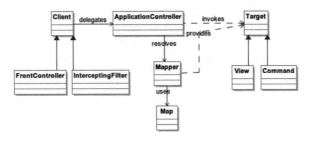

Figure 7-27   Application Controller pattern diagram

Benefits

The following lists the benefits of using the Application Controller pattern:

- Improves extensibility
- Improves separation of concerns

When to Use

You should use the Application Controller pattern to:

- Apply common control logic
- Have centralized view management

View Helper

The View Helper pattern separates the processing logic from the view. Figure 7-28 illustrates the View Helper pattern.

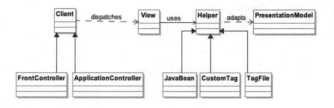

Figure 7-28   View Helper pattern diagram

Benefits

The following is a benefit of using the View Helper pattern:

■ Separates logic from the view

When to Use

You should use the View Helper pattern to:

■ Encapsulate view-processing logic

Composite View

The Composite View pattern combines simple views into a more complex view without handling the content or layout. Figure 7-29 illustrates the Composite View pattern.

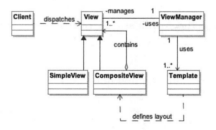

Figure 7-29   Composite View pattern diagram

Benefits

The following lists the benefits of using the Composite View pattern:

- Code duplication is reduced because you can create common headers, footers, and other components.
- Views can be changed based on access authorization.

When to Use

You should use the Composite View pattern when:

- You want common view components.
- You view component changes based on authorization.

Dispatcher View

The Dispatcher View pattern handles the request and generates a response while managing limited business processing. Figure 7-30 illustrates the Dispatcher View pattern.

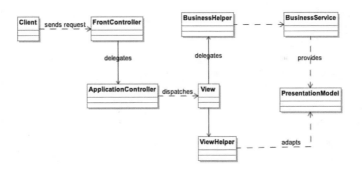

Figure 7-30   Dispatcher View pattern diagram

Benefits

The following lists the benefits of using the Dispatcher View pattern:

- Separates processing logic from view
- Improves reusability

When to Use

You should use the Dispatcher View pattern when:

- You have static views.
- You have limited business processing.

Service to Worker

The Service to Worker pattern performs request handling and invokes business logic before control is passed to the view. Figure 7-31 illustrates the Service to Worker pattern.

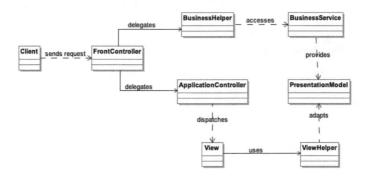

Figure 7-31   Service to Worker pattern diagram

Benefits

The following is a benefit of using the Service to Worker pattern:

- Improves separation of concerns

When to Use

You should use the Service to Worker pattern to:

- Centralize business logic for requests

Business Tier

Business tier patterns create a loose coupling among the business logic, presentation, and resources.

Business Delegate

The Business Delegate pattern hides the complexity of remote communication with business components from the client. Figure 7-32 illustrates the Business Delegate pattern.

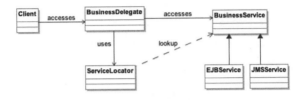

Figure 7-32   Business Delegate pattern diagram

Benefits

The following lists the benefits of using the Business Delegate pattern:

- Minimizes coupling of clients to business services
- Hides remoteness
- Improves performance

When to Use

You should use the Business Delegate pattern when you:

- Want to encapsulate access to business services from multiple client types
- Translate exceptions into application exceptions
- Hide details of service creation

Service Locator

The Service Locator pattern uses a consistent approach to locating business components regardless of the type of components. Figure 7-33 illustrates the Service Locator pattern.

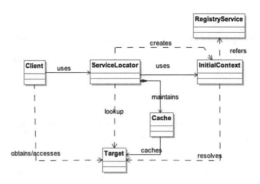

Figure 7-33   Service Locator pattern diagram

Benefits

The following is a benefit of using the Service Locator pattern:

- Standardized approach to retrieving business components

When to Use

You should use the Service Locator pattern when:

- You have many different business services that are located in different ways.

Session Façade

The Session Façade pattern provides a coarse-grained service of business components to remote clients. This is the same as a Façade pattern, but just provides an interface to a service instead of code. Figure 7-34 illustrates the Session Façade pattern.

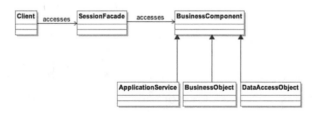

Figure 7-34   Session Façade pattern diagram

Benefits

The following lists the benefits of using the Session Facade pattern:

- Reduces the number of calls to the business component from the client
- Reduces coupling between the tiers
- Improves performance by reducing fine-grained calls from client
- Provides a cleaner API to the client

When to Use

You should use the Session Facade pattern when:

- You have a series of calls to make to business components from the client.

Application Service

The Application Service pattern centralizes and aggregates business components. An application service could be thought of as a helper to the Session Façade that takes care of all the business logic and workflow. Figure 7-35 illustrates the Application Service pattern.

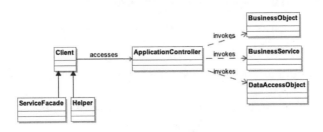

Figure 7-35 Application Service pattern diagram

Benefits

The following lists the benefits of using the Application Service pattern:

- Centralizes and improves reusability of business logic
- Simplifies the Session Façade by eliminating the business logic

When to Use

You should use the Application Service pattern when you:

- Start to see duplicated business logic in the Session Façade

Business Object

The Business Object pattern separates business data from logic. Figure 7-36 illustrates the Business Object pattern.

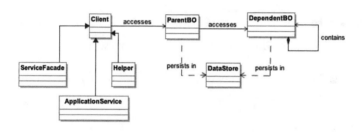

Figure 7-36   Business Object pattern diagram

Benefits

The following is a benefit of using the Business Object pattern:
- Separates persistence from business logic.

When to Use

You should use the Business Object pattern when you:

- Want to increase reusability of business logic.

Composite Entity

The Composite Entity pattern aggregates business entities into a coarse-grained entity. Figure 7-37 illustrates the Composite Entity pattern.

Benefits

The following lists the benefits of using the Composite Entity pattern:

- Increases maintainability
- Improves network performance

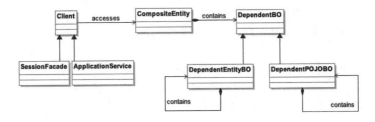

Figure 7-37   Composite Entity pattern diagram

When to Use

You should use the Composite Entity pattern to:

- Avoid remote entity beans
- Leverage bean managed persistence (BMP) with custom persistence implementation
- Encapsulate POJO business objects

Transfer Object

The Transfer Object pattern uses an object to carry data across tiers. Figure 7-38 illustrates the Transfer Object pattern.

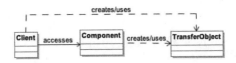

Figure 7-38   Transfer Object pattern diagram

Benefits

The following lists the benefits of using the Transfer Object pattern:

- Reduces network traffic
- Reduces code duplication

When to Use

You should use the Transfer Object pattern when:

- You need to send objects between tiers.

Transfer Object Assembler

The Transfer Object Assembler pattern builds a composite transfer object and returns to the client. Figure 7-39 illustrates the Transfer Object Assembler.

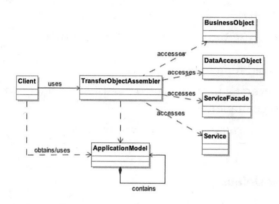

Figure 7-39   Transfer Object Assembler pattern diagram

Benefits

The following is a benefit of using the Transfer Object Assembler pattern:

- Improves network performance

When to Use

You should use the Transfer Object Assembler pattern when:

- You have several transfer objects that are sent between tiers.

Value List Handler

The Value List Handler pattern caches results and allows the client to traverse and select from the results. Figure 7-40 illustrates the Value List Handler pattern.

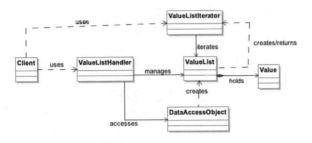

Figure 7-40   Value List Handler pattern diagram

Benefits

The following lists the benefits of using the Value List Handler pattern:

- Caches search results
- Improves network performance
- Improves separation of concerns

When to Use

You should use the Value List Handler pattern when you:

- Want to iterate through a set of objects.
- Implement read-only lists without transactions.

Integration Tier

Integration tier patterns are used to isolate the core business logic of the system from the external systems or data stores.

Data Access Object

The Data Access Object pattern encapsulates access to a persistent store by managing the connection with the data store. Figure 7-41 illustrates the Data Access Object pattern.

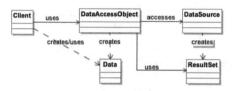

Figure 7-41   Data Access Object pattern diagram

Benefits

The following lists the benefits of using the Data Access Object pattern:

- Reduces code complexity in client
- Improves code reuse
- Provides easier migration to new data store

When to Use

You should use the Data Access Object pattern to:

- Decouple data access from the business logic
- Provide all data access from in a separate layer

Service Activator

The Service Activator pattern handles asynchronous requests to business components. Figure 7-42 illustrates the Service Activator pattern.

Benefits

The following lists the benefits of using the Service Activator pattern:

- Allows the client to continue processing
- Integrates JMS into application

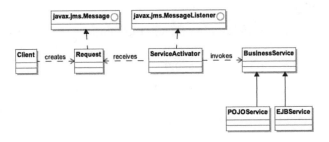

Figure 7-42   Service Activator pattern diagram

When to Use

You should use the Service Activator pattern when:

■ You need to invoke a business service in an asynchronous manner.

Domain Store

The Domain Store pattern separates the persistence of an object from the object model. This pattern really became relevant with the advent of object relational model frameworks and products. You would use the domain store and data access object at the same time. Figure 7-43 illustrates the Domain Store pattern.

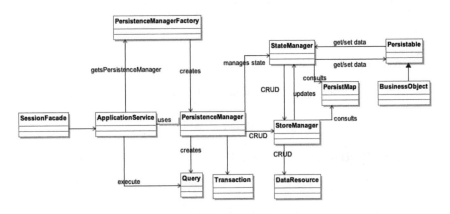

Figure 7-43   Domain Store pattern diagram

Benefits

The following is a benefit of using the Domain Store pattern:

- Decouples business logic from persistence logic

When to Use

You should use the Domain Store pattern when:

- You do not want to use entity beans.
- Object model uses are complex.

Web Service Broker

The Web Service Broker pattern exposes and brokers services using XML and web protocols. Figure 7-44 illustrates the Web Service Broker pattern.

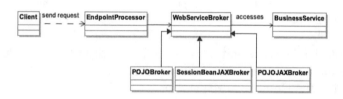

Figure 7-44   Web Service Broker pattern diagram

Benefits

The following is a benefit of using the Web Service Broker pattern:

- Exposes existing services to web

When to Use

You should use the Web Service Broker pattern when you:

- Need to expose services as web services

Essential Points

The following summarizes the most important points described in this chapter:

- Creational patterns allow objects to be created in a system without having to identify a specific class type in the code, so you do not have to write large, complex code to instantiate an object.

- The Abstract Factory pattern provides an interface for creating families of related or dependent objects without specifying their concrete classes.

- The Builder pattern separates the construction of a complex object from its representation so the same construction process can create different objects.

- The Factory Method pattern defines an interface for creating an object, but lets the subclasses decide which class to instantiate.

- The Prototype pattern allows an object to create customized objects without knowing their exact class or the details of how to create them.

- The Singleton pattern ensures that a class has only one instance, and provides a global point of access to that class.

- Structural patterns control the relationships between large portions of your applications.

- The Adapter pattern acts as an intermediary between two classes, converting the interface of one class so that it can be used with the other.

- The Bridge pattern divides a complex component into two separate but related inheritance hierarchies: the functional abstraction and the internal implementation.

- The Composite pattern enables you to create hierarchical tree structures of varying complexity, while allowing every element in the structure to operate with a uniform interface.

- The Decorator pattern enables you to add or remove object functionality without changing the external appearance or function of the object.

- The Façade pattern provides a unified interface to a group of interfaces in a subsystem.

- The Flyweight pattern reduces the number of low-level, detailed objects within a system by sharing objects.

- The Proxy pattern provides a surrogate or placeholder object to control access to the original object.

- Behavioral patterns influence how state and behavior flow through a system.

- The Chain of Responsibility pattern establishes a chain within a system, so that a message can either be handled at the level where it is first received, or be directed to an object that can handle it.

- The Command pattern encapsulates a request in an object, which enables you to store the command, pass the command to a method, and return the command like any other object.

- The Interpreter pattern interprets a language to define a representation for its grammar along with an interpreter that uses the representation to interpret sentences in the language.

- The Iterator pattern provides a consistent way to sequentially access items in a collection that is independent of and separate from the underlying collection.

- The Mediator pattern simplifies communication among objects in a system by introducing a single object that manages message distribution among other objects.

- The Memento pattern preserves a "snapshot" of an object's state, so that the object can return to its original state without having to reveal its content to the rest of the world

- The Observer pattern provides a way for a component to flexibly broadcast messages to interested receivers.

- The State pattern allows an object to alter its behavior when its internal state changes.

- The Strategy pattern defines a group of classes that represent a set of possible behaviors.

- The Template Method pattern provides a method that allows subclasses to override parts of the method without rewriting it.

- The Visitor pattern provides a maintainable, easy way to represent an operation to be performed on the elements of an object structure.

- The Intercepting Filter pattern provides the ability to manipulate a request prior to processing or to manipulate the response before sending the results of the request.

- The Context Object pattern is used to encapsulate the specifics of protocol implementation to be shared.

- The Front Controller pattern creates central control logic for presentation request handling. The Front Controller is different from the Intercepting Filter in that the Front Controller is determining processing based on the request and an Intercepting Filter is modifying the request.

- The Application Controller pattern is used to centralize retrieval and invocation of request-processing components, such as commands and views.

- The View Helper pattern separates the processing logic from the view.

- The Composite View pattern combines simple views into a more complex view without handling the content or layout.

- The Dispatcher View pattern handles the request and generates a response while managing limited business processing.

- The Service to Worker pattern performs request handling and invokes business logic before control is passed to the view.

- The Business Delegate pattern hides the complexity of remote communication with business components from the client.

- The Service Locator pattern uses a consistent approach to locating business components regardless of the type of components.

- The Session Façade patterns provides a coarse-grained service of business components to remote clients. This is the same as a Façade pattern, but just provides an interface to a service instead of code.

- The Application Service pattern centralizes and aggregates business components. An application service could be thought of as a helper to the Session Façade that takes care of all the business logic and workflow.

- The Business Object pattern separates business data from logic.

- The Composite Entity pattern aggregates business entities into a coarse-grained entity.

- The Transfer Object pattern uses an object to carry data across tiers.
- The Transfer Object Assembler pattern builds a composite transfer object and returns to the client.
- The Value List Handler pattern caches results and allows the client to traverse and select from the results.
- The Data Access Object pattern encapsulates access to a persistent store by managing the connection with the data store.
- The Service Activator pattern handles asynchronous requests to business components.
- The Domain Store pattern separates the persistence of an object from the object model. This pattern really became relevant with the advent of object relational model frameworks and products. You would use the domain store and data access object at the same time.
- The Web Service Broker pattern exposes and brokers services using XML and web protocols.

Review Your Progress

This section reviews the objectives described in the chapter and provides review questions to ensure that you understand the chapter's important points:

1. Which pattern would you use to create a complex object and have the assembly and parts independent?

   A. Prototype
   B. Singleton
   C. Builder
   D. Abstract Factory

   Answer: C. The Builder pattern enables you to create complex objects and keep the parts and the assembling of those parts separate and independent.

2. You are asked to interface with a class in an existing system, but the interface does not match the interface you need. Which pattern would you use?

   A. Decorator
   B. Abstract Factory
   C. Command
   D. Adapter

   Answer: D. The Adapter pattern enables you to adapt the interface of a class or component to meet your needs.

3. What are two benefits of the Façade pattern? (Choose two.)

   A. It hides complex subsystems from clients.
   B. It allows objects to masquerade as different objects.
   C. It decouples the object interface from the implementation.
   D. It encourages weak coupling between the client and the subsystem.

   Answers: A and D. The Façade pattern hides complex subsystems from clients and encourages weak coupling between the client and the subsystem.

4. What are two benefits of the Singleton pattern? (Choose two.)

   A. It encourages use of global variables.
   B. It controls access to a single instance.
   C. It permits a variable number of instances.
   D. It allows a collection of objects to be manipulated as a single object.

   Answers: B and C. The Singleton pattern controls access to a single instance or a variable number of instances.

5. A company created its own MVC-like framework in the years before Struts and JSF. Unfortunately, the company Front Controller has become bloated with too many features, including fine-grained authorization, view dispatching, and business logic invocation.

Which three patterns could be applied to reduce the complexity of this Front Controller? (Choose three.)

A. Mediator

B. Command

C. View Helper

D. Intercepting Filter

E. Composite View

F. Application Controller

Answers: B, C, and F. Application Controller will help with view management and dispatching. Intercepting Filter can handle the authorization. The Command pattern will encapsulate the business logic.

CHAPTER 8

Documenting an Architecture

- Document a given system architecture by creating UML diagrams for it.
- Create a logical and physical model of a system infrastructure architecture.

Introduction

There are many ways to communicate the architecture to the development team. The de-facto industry standard is a set of UML diagrams. We will explain the different UML diagrams that can be used to communicate the architecture and discuss when it is appropriate to use each diagram. Remember that the key focus of an architect is to communicate the architecture to the developers.

This chapter will introduce material that is relevant to the assignment portion of the exam. There are no multiple choice questions in this chapter. If you are already familiar with UML notation and documenting an architecture, feel free to move to the next chapter.

Prerequisite Review

It is expected that you already have a general understanding of the different diagrams in UML. We will quickly review the different UML diagrams and then discuss which diagrams are pertinent to documenting an architecture. We will not be covering the specific notation of the diagrams.

If you do not meet the prerequisites, review the following resources to gain the appropriate level of knowledge before proceeding:

- http://en.wikipedia.org/wiki/Unified_Modeling_Language
- *UML Distilled: A Brief Guide to the Standard Object Modeling Language* by Martin Fowler
- *Learning UML 2.0* by Russ Miles and Kim Hamilton

Discussion

The purpose of creating an architecture is to communicate the overall system structure to the development team so they can build the system within the constraints and guidelines provided. Most of the communication of the architecture can be accomplished with UML diagrams.

What is a model? A **model** is a simplification of reality. You build models using UML diagrams to better understand the system you are developing. The models you build will help you do the following:

- Visualize the system as it is or as you want it to be
- Specify the structure or behavior of a system
- Provide a template to guide the construction of the system
- Document the decisions made about the system

To start modeling with the UML, you need to learn the three major elements of the UML: building blocks, rules for combining building blocks, and common mechanisms. Once you have mastered the three elements, you can read and create UML diagrams.

Building Blocks of UML

There are three types of building blocks: elements, relationships, and diagrams. **Elements** are the abstractions that are first-class citizens in a model; **relationships** tie these elements together; and **diagrams** group collections of related elements by means of relationships.

Elements

There are four kinds of elements in UML, as follows:

- **Structural**—Used to create the static parts of a model by representing elements that are conceptual or physical
- **Behavioral**—Enables you to model the behavior of the system
- **Grouping**—Enables you to organize the structural and behavioral elements in your model
- **Annotational**—Explanatory parts of the model

These elements are the basic elements used in creating models.

Structural Elements

There are seven structural elements: class, interface, collaboration, use case, active class, component, and node. The four that are most pertinent to documenting an architecture, as follows:

- A **class** is a set of objects that share the same attributes, operations, relationships, and semantics. The class is represented by a rectangle with three areas. The first area contains the name of the class, the second area contains the attributes of the class, and the third contains the operations of the class. Figure 8-1 illustrates a class.

Figure 8-1   Example of a class

- The **interface** is a collection of operations that specify a service of a class or component. The interface is represented by a rectangle with the same three areas as the class. An interface has the

addition of the word "interface" above the interface name to identify it as an interface. Figure 8-2 illustrates an interface.

Figure 8-2   Example of an interface

- A **component** is a physical and replaceable part of a system that
  conforms to and provides the realization of a set of interfaces.
  Visually, the component is a rectangle with two prongs so that it
  appears that it could be plugged into something. Figure 8-3 illustrates a component.

Figure 8-3   Example of a component

- A **node** is a physical element that exists at run time and represents a computational resource, generally having at least some
  memory and often processing capability. Visually, the node looks
  like a cube with a name on the front side of the cube. Figure 8-4
  illustrates a node.

Figure 8-4   Example of a node

Behavioral Elements

Behavioral elements are used to model the behavior of a system. There
are two types of behaviors as follows:

- **Interaction** is a type of behavior element that comprises a set of messages exchanged among a set of objects within a particular context to accomplish a specific purpose. An interaction is represented by a solid arrow line. Figure 8-5 illustrates an arrow.

Figure 8-5   Example of an interaction

- A **state machine** is a type of behavior that specifies the sequence of states an object or an interaction goes through during its lifetime in response to events, together with its responses to those events. Figure 8-6 illustrates a state machine.

Figure 8-6   Example of a state

Grouping Element

There is only one type of grouping element—a package. A **package** is a general-purpose mechanism for organizing elements into groups. Figure 8-7 illustrates a package.

Figure 8-7   Example of a package

Annotational Elements

There is only one type of annotational element, called a note. A **note** is a symbol for rendering comments that you want attached to other elements or collections of elements. Visually, the note is represented by a rectangle with the upper-right corner folded in. Figure 8-8 illustrates a note.

Figure 8-8   Example of a note

Relationships

There are four standard relationships in UML: dependency, association, generalization, and realization. We will not cover realization here because it is more of a analysis relationship. You use the relationships to create links between the elements in your model, as follows:

■ A **dependency** is a semantic relationship between two elements in which a change to one thing (the independent thing) can affect the semantics of the other thing (the dependent thing). The dependency is represented as a dashed-line with an arrow on the end. The arrow indicates the direction of the dependency. Using the following diagram, Class1 has a reference to Class2, either passed as a method parameter or defined as a method variable in some method. Figure 8-9 illustrates a dependency relationship.

Figure 8-9   Example of a dependency

■ **Aggregation** is a special kind of association, representing a structural relationship between a whole and its parts. The Aggregation association is a diagram with an open diamond on the side of the whole. Using Figure 8-9, we can see that a Company as the whole is comprised of its parts, which is the Employees. Figure 8-10 illustrates an aggregation.

Figure 8-10   Example of aggregation

- **Generalization** is a specialization/generalization relationship in which objects of the specialized element (child) are substitutable for objects of the generalized element (parent). Generalization is visually represented as a line with an open arrow on the end. The arrow points from the child/subclass to the parent/superclass. Figure 8-11 illustrates a generalization.

Figure 8-11   Example of generalization

Common Mechanisms

There are four common mechanisms that apply consistently throughout UML: specifications, adornments, common division, and extensibility.

Specifications

UML is more than just a graphical language. Behind every part of its graphical notation, there is a specification that provides a textual statement of the syntax and the semantics of that building block. For example, a class icon has a specification that provides the full set of attributes, operations, and behaviors embodied by that class. Visually, a class icon might show only a small part of the specification, or it might show the entire class specification. With this in mind, you could create diagrams with only icons and build up the specification, or you could create the specification by reverse engineering and then build up the diagrams. Figure 8-12 contains the -attribute1:int and +operation1():void, which are the specifications of the class name.

Adornments

The adornments mechanism indicates whether an element is public, private, or protected, and represented by +, -, and #, respectively. In the previous example, attribute1 is private and operation1 is public.

Common Divisions

The common division mechanism designates instances of an element. For example, if the element name is underlined, it is an instance of an element. You can precede an element name with a : and have an anonymous instance. You can place a name in front of the : and have a named instance of an element. Figure 8-12 contains the :name, which means that you have an anonymous instance of class name.

Figure 8-12   Example of Anonymous class with specifications and adornments

Extensibility Mechanisms

Extensibility mechanisms enable you to shape and grow UML to meet your project's requirements. In addition, these mechanisms enable UML to adapt quickly to new technologies by creating new building blocks from the existing UML building blocks:

- **Stereotypes**—Extends the vocabulary of UML, enabling you to create new kinds of building blocks. These building blocks are derived from existing building blocks but are specific to your problem.

- **Tagged values**—Extends the properties of a UML building block, enabling you to create new information in that element's specification.

- **Constraints**—Extends the semantics of a UML building block, enabling you to add new rules or modify existing ones.

UML Diagrams

UML has two main categories of diagrams: structure and behavior. Behavior diagrams have a subcategory called interaction diagrams. **Structure diagrams** describe the components that make up the system. **Behavior diagrams** describe the processing of the system, and **interaction diagrams** describe the flow of control and data among the system components.

Structure Diagrams

Structure diagrams are used to communicate the overall structure of the system to the developers.

Class Diagram

A **class diagram** shows a set of classes, interfaces, and collaborations and their relationships. These diagrams are the most common diagrams found in modeling object-oriented systems. Class diagrams address the static design view of a system. Class diagrams that include active classes address the static process view of a system.

Figure 8-13 shows nine classes. Two of the classes, Buy and Sell, are subclasses of the superclass Transaction. This diagram tells us that a customer can have one cash account and many portfolios. A portfolio has many accounts, an account has many holdings, and a holding has one stock and can be accessed by many transactions. The holding does not know which transactions are associated to it, because of the navigability. Each transaction can have only one holding and one cash account. The transaction can be of type Buy or Sell.

A domain-level class diagram can be useful in showing the developers the domain objects and their relationships, thus providing constraints and system boundaries. Class diagrams can also show the classes of a component and how those classes are related.

Component Diagram

A **component diagram** shows the organizations and dependencies among a set of components. Component diagrams address the static implementation view of a system. They are related to class diagrams in that a component diagram typically maps to one or more classes, interfaces, or collaborations.

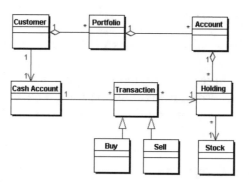

Figure 8-13   Example class diagram

Figure 8-14 uses stereotypes to create new J2EE-specific components of JSP, Servlet, and SessionBean. The Search component sends requests to the SearchController component, which makes a request to the SearchEngine and sends the results to the SearchResults JSP. The SearchEngine component uses the ICatalog interface to retrieve information from the Catalog subsystem.

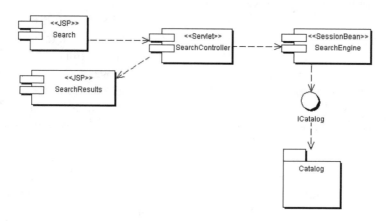

Figure 8-14   Example component diagram

Component diagrams are used to communicate the overall pattern for the system. Each system has a basic pattern that developers should follow, such as MVC or DAO for all database access.

Deployment Diagram

A **deployment diagram** shows the configuration of run-time processing nodes and the components that live on these nodes. Deployment diagrams address the static deployment view of an architecture. They are related to component diagrams in that a node typically encloses one or more components.

Figure 8-15 shows a four-node system configuration. The browser uses HTTP to communicate with the web server, which runs the Search-Controller Servlet, Search JSP, and SearchResults JSP. The web server uses RMI to communicate with the application server, which runs the search engine session bean. The application server uses IIOP to communicate with the Catalog System node.

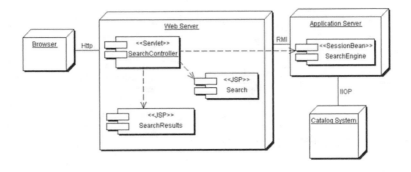

Figure 8-15   Example deployment diagram

Deployment diagrams help the developers to understand the boundaries of the system components and what protocol they will use to communicate with dependent components.

Package Diagram

A **package diagram** is a special kind of class diagram. Package diagrams represent the organization of the system in groups. You could use a package diagram to show the physical packages you expect within the system.

Figure 8-16 uses the stereotype <<subsystem>> to define the package to be a subsystem. This package diagram is really a subsystem diagram that shows the subsystems of the system and the dependencies between the subsystems. For example, the CustomerProfile subsystem needs the Security subsystem and is used by the OrderEntry and Marketing subsystems.

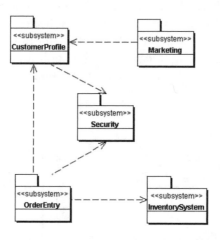

Figure 8-16   Example package diagram

Package diagrams are used to communicate the packaging of the software for build and deployment.

Behavior Diagrams

Behavior diagrams are used to communicate the detailed processing of the system and interaction of components.

Activity Diagram

An **activity diagram** is a special kind of a statechart diagram that shows the flow from activity to activity within a system. An activity diagram addresses the dynamic view of a system. This type of diagram is important in modeling the function of a system and emphasizing the flow of control among objects.

Figure 8-17 starts with Activity1 and then creates parallel execution to Activity2 and Activity3. Activity2 has two possible outcomes. If Activity2 fails, proceed to Activity4 and exit. If Activity2 succeeds, proceed to Activity5 and join with the parallel execution from Activity3. After Activity3 and Activity5 are joined, execution continues with Activity6 and then completes.

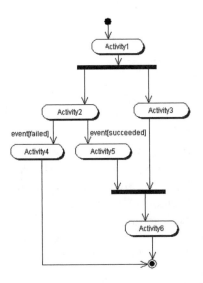

Figure 8-17   Example activity diagram

Statechart Diagram

A **statechart diagram** shows a state machine consisting of states, transitions, events, and activities. Statechart diagrams address the dynamic view of a system. They are important in modeling the behavior of an interface, class, or collaboration, and emphasize the event-ordered behavior of an object, which is useful in modeling reactive systems.

Figure 8-18 represents the state of a reservation. Initially, the reservation is on hold and proceeds to a booking state. If successful, the state of the reservation is booked; if the booking fails, the reservation is cancelled.

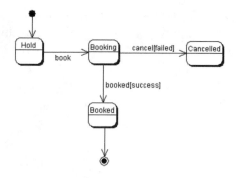

Figure 8-18   Example statechart diagram

Use-Case Diagram

A **use-case diagram** shows a set of use cases and actors and their relationships. Use-case diagrams address the static use-case view of a system. These diagrams are especially important in organizing and modeling the behaviors of a system.

Figure 8-19 has actors Customer, Catalog System, Service Rep, and Warehouse. The Customer and Service Rep actors interact with the use-cases Browse Catalog, Search for Product, Create Customer Account, and Checkout. The Browse Catalog and Search for Product use cases retrieve or send information to the Catalog System actor. The Checkout use case retrieves or sends information to the Warehouse actor.

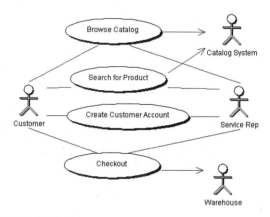

Figure 8-19   Example use-case diagram

Interaction Diagrams

Both sequence and collaboration diagrams are kinds of interaction diagrams. An **interaction diagram** shows an interaction, consisting of a set of objects and their relationships, including the messages that can be dispatched among them. Interaction diagrams address the dynamic view of a system. A **sequence diagram** is an interaction diagram that emphasizes the time ordering of messages; a **collaboration diagram** is an interaction diagram that emphasizes the structural organization of the objects that send and receive messages. Sequence and collaboration diagrams are isomorphic, meaning that you can take one and transform it into the other.

All interaction diagrams start with an actor. Figures 8-20 and 8-21 show the Actor sending a start message to the Start Object, which sends a Create to Object1, which sends a Create to Object2. Object2 sends a loadData message to itself, which is a recursive message. Object2 then returns to Object1, which returns to Start Object. There are no return arrows, as returns in interaction diagrams are implicit. The two diagrams are modeling the same flow of events. To understand the flow of events on a collaboration diagram, the messages are numbered, making it easier to follow.

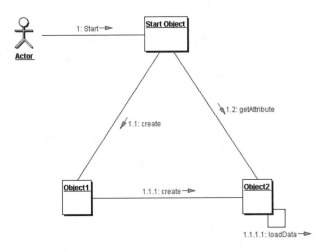

Figure 8-20   Communication diagram (also known as a collaboration diagram)

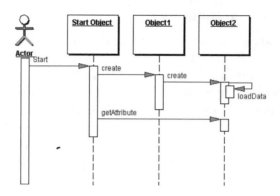

Figure 8-21   Sequence diagram

Interaction diagrams are useful to communicate flow of events between objects. This can be very useful with complex interactions.

Essential Points

- UML diagrams are used to communicate the system architecture to the developers. As an architect, you will need to understand the different types of diagrams and make a determination as to which diagram will communicate the knowledge to the developers.
- Structure diagrams, such as class, component, deployment, and package diagrams, are useful when communicating the overall structure of the system.
- Behavior diagrams, such as activity, statechart, use-case, communication, and sequence diagrams, are used to communicate the unusual processing of the system.

Review Your Progress

Because this chapter is only pertinent to the assignment, there are no review questions. Your assignment submission will be graded on how clearly you communicate your architecture to the assessors and how clear and easy the diagrams are to read. The assignment requests the following diagrams be created for your submission: class diagram, component diagram, deployment diagram, and interaction diagrams. Chapter 9, "Tackling Parts II and III," provides a documented example of the assignment.

CHAPTER 9

Tackling Parts II and III

There are no specific exam objectives to quote for this chapter—all the exam objectives already covered apply equally to the material addressed here.

Introduction

This chapter is distinct from the other chapters in that it deals with the exam itself—specifically, how to prepare for and answer Parts II and III.

Simply put, Part II of the exam requires you, the candidate, to propose a JEE-based solution to a given business problem scenario. Once you have completed and submitted this assignment, Part III poses a series of questions to you designed to probe the strengths and weaknesses of your solution to basic application functional and non-functional characteristics.

Therefore, in this chapter, we present a specific scenario similar in complexity to that you can expect to receive in the exam itself, and then present our own solution to it. Having completed that, we then move on to consider the obvious functional and non-functional questions that can be asked of that assignment.

Prerequisite Review

There are no specific prerequisites for this chapter.

Discussion

In this section, we present a scenario on a par with the complexity that you can expect to receive in the actual exam and then our own proposed solution to that scenario.

Scenario

You are the architect for JustBuildIt Corporation, an international, vertically integrated construction company with significant operations in the U.S. and Canada, Europe, and the Pacific Rim. JustBuildIt operates its own forests, quarries, and steel foundries to supply its own building sites with wood, concrete, and steel. This end-to-end style of operation has helped JustBuildIt to keep down its costs of raw material in an era of soaring commodity prices, but equally has forced it to build and maintain a complex back office and distribution network—eroding a significant portion of those cost savings. The management team has recently concluded a business-wide review, from leaves to roots, of the entire company, and one fact is apparent—JustBuildIt pays a lot of money moving raw materials to construction sites, even when there are materials just as suitable nearby.

JustBuildIt has decided to build a building commodities exchange to allow both it and some of its competitors to effectively pool excess capacity in a co-opetition model. In the future, raw materials for a given construction job will be sourced through the exchange, rather than exclusively from JustBuildIt inventory. (Although, of course, excess JustBuildIt inventory will be prioritized for use over another company's inventory.) Based on the management's report and also interviews with key senior staff, you know the following:

- JustBuildIt has recently invested in an inventory and order management system, which tracks both capacity of their production facilities and also individual orders coming in from construction sites around the world. This system is accessed via a JMS queue.

- JustBuildIt has decided to expose the interface to their exchange as a web services API.

- In order to counter accusations of unfairness, JustBuildIt has agreed with all participants that 95% of all transactions to and from the exchange will execute in 5 seconds or less, with the remaining 5% executing in 20 seconds or less.

- The system has an uptime requirement during core working hours (GMT -8 to GMT +8) of 99.99%.

- The actual placement of orders into the exchange is a manual process—inventory managers place excess product capacity into the system manually, allowing site managers to place bids for the product they want, with the most competitive bid winning the auction process.

The domain model shown in Figure 9-1 details the main business objects that describe the overall system. This model, along with the use-case diagram, represents the pictorial description of the business problem to which you must provide a solution for Parts II and III of the exam.

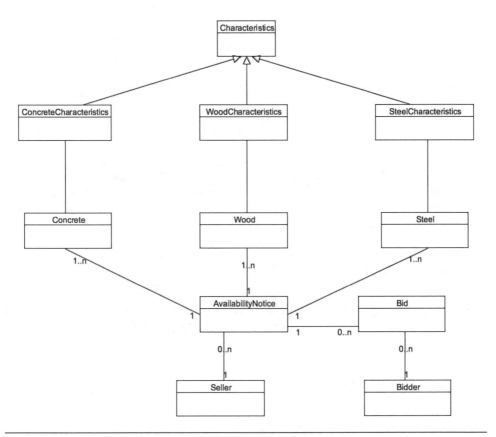

Figure 9-1   Business domain model for the JustBuildIt scenario

The use cases for the business scenario (detailed in Figure 9-2) describe the specific business operations that must be supported in your proposed solution. Although they can be thought of as influencing just the sequence diagram deliverable directly, the use cases should also be used to evaluate the class and component diagrams to ensure that your solution as a whole supports each use case. Some of the exam scenarios contain more than the three use cases described here; however, the complexity is equivalent.

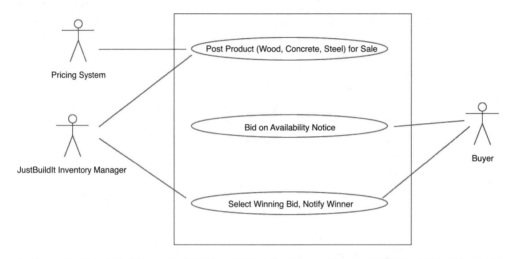

Figure 9-2   The three use cases for the JustBuildIt scenario that must be addressed in your solution

Worked Solution

In this section, we will detail exactly the same thought processes that you should apply to your own solution and apply them in turn to the Just-BuildIt scenario.

Class Diagram

This may sound obvious, but ensure that all the objects detailed in the domain model are present in your class diagram. You may spot a more efficient or elegant representation of relationships, attributes, or behavior, and within reason feel free to express your superior design, but remember: This is a contrived exam scenario, not a workshop where you can win client buy-in to your improved approach. You cannot influence the examiner when he or she is correcting your assignment—therefore, missing information means missing marks. Another common mistake (in all diagrams, not just the class diagram) is to focus on the "how" and not the "what." Simply put: Yes, you should select and commit to a method or framework that describes how you plan to build the System under Development (SuD) at the web/presentation, business logic, persistence, and integration tiers, but this focus on the "how" must not be at the expense of the "what." Here is a simple test to ensure that your class diagram captures the *business IPR* of JustBuildIt—explain it to yourself out loud: Name every class starting with the most important and traverse the entire class diagram using the relationships, explaining the cardinality as you go. This simple procedure will simultaneously ensure that you stay on track and focus on the solution and also make you annoying to people near you—a win-win situation. Figure 9-3 takes the domain model and develops it into the associated class diagram. There are some important points to note on the class diagram, as follows:

- The class diagram remains web framework agnostic. Any web framework (within reason) is an acceptable choice—we merely assume a standard MVC separation of concerns.

- Just as importantly, the web framework and persistence plumbing is not allowed to detract from the domain model classes themselves. The relationships and interplays are important and should not be ignored, but equally the primary purpose of the class diagram is to show your conversion of the domain model into a functioning class diagram *that solves the business problem.*

- Colors have not been used to impart information—but if you choose to use colors in your class diagram (or any of the exam deliverables), you must provide a color key explaining clearly what the colors stand for.

- Annotations have been used to show the examiner how specific items in the domain model have been mapped onto JEE components—specifically, session beans and Entity classes.

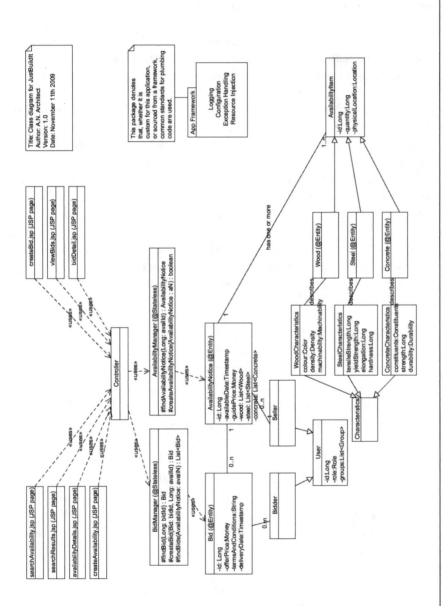

Figure 9-3 The class diagram is developed from the domain model and models elements as entities or session beans, as well as reorganizing the elements into a classic n-tier layered architecture.

Component Diagram

The component diagram is another view of the system, at a higher level than the class diagram. In this view, you are expected to demonstrate the ability to visualize the system at a higher level and understand (and illustrate clearly) all of the moving parts in your solution. If you have proposed an innovative use of MDBs to solve a particularly thorny integration issue, here is where you need to depict and justify that decision. Figure 9-4 depicts the component diagram for the JustBuildIt solution.

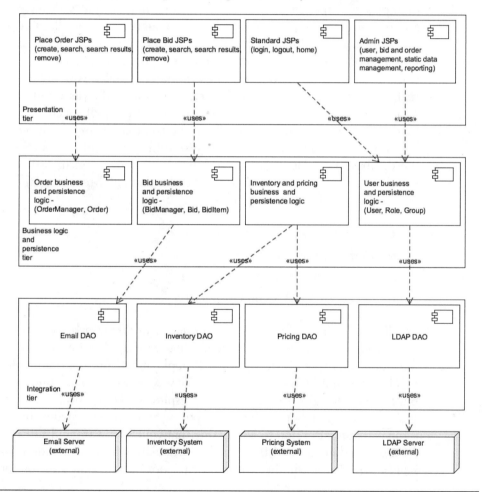

Figure 9-4   The component diagram builds further on the class diagram, grouping logically related classes together into components that carry out a distinct business operation. Moreover, the component diagram is laid out so as to make the layered nature of the architecture clear to the examiner.

Deployment Diagram

The deployment diagram captures information about how you intend that the system operate in production—both logically and physically. There is little point in naming specific machines, vendors, or routers, as these decisions change so quickly. However, do indicate in a vendor/machine-agnostic way the resources you expect to be deployed in order to support your architecture—CPUs, RAM, network requirements, disk configuration, and so on—and then provide concrete examples of a specific vendor/machine combination that satisfies your theoretical capacity prediction. Significant marks are not allocated to this information (although marks are indeed allocated), but it does impress upon the examiner that you have considered the hardware and software needed in a production environment to make your solution a reality. Figure 9-5 lays out a deployment diagram for the JustBuildIt system. In this diagram, we have adopted the convention of specifying two hardware profiles (A and B) to call out the fact that we expect the combined web/application servers to require different system resources to the database tier. Although the resources deemed necessary will vary from one exam scenario to the next, the fundamental resources themselves will not. These are as follows:

- CPUs (number of cores, clock speed)
- RAM (quantity in GB)
- Network (minimum interface speed)
- Storage (disk/SAN configuration)

Finally, at the time of writing (third quarter of 2009), a brief word on cloud computing. Feel free to specify that your application will run in the cloud and explicitly design for that deployment. But the exam deliverables must not be compromised in any way. For example, cloud computing does not give free scalability (despite marketing propaganda to the contrary). Neither is cloud computing free. You must devote the same care and attention to addressing that your hardware and software solution is adequate and that you can articulate why your solution will scale and perform, whether you choose to adopt cloud computing or not.

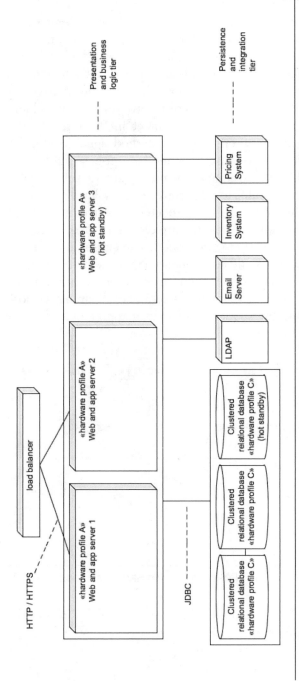

Figure 9-5 The deployment diagram depicts how the proposed solution will execute at runtime, including suggesting the likely hardware and configuration that will be needed to support the software solution.

Sequence Diagrams

There's not much to say about sequence diagrams. They are pretty boring and tedious to draw, they are often the first diagram that gets out of sync with the concrete implementation of the design, and they are a necessary part of the exam. You must supply a sequence or collaboration diagram for each specified use case. Do not roll one or more use cases together into a single diagram for brevity or to save time—you will lose marks. There is also a clear area of disconnect in the exam that is exposed here. You are not required to supply method signatures for any of the classes you define, yet you are expected to supply sequence diagrams. Because of this, the examiner is not going to submit your sequence/collaboration diagrams to a rigorous compiler-level of correctness and syntax checking. What you are expected to deliver and will be examined for are sequence diagrams that are clear and broadly map to the complexity of the use case being described. The classes and components you created in the class and component diagram should be represented, along with the calls between them necessary to implement the use case being documented. Trivially simple sequence diagrams will lose marks. Figure 9-6 shows the sequence diagram mapping onto the first use case: post product for sale.

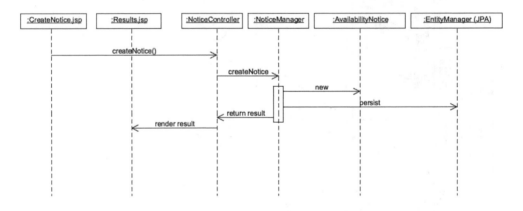

Figure 9-6   The sequence diagram for the "Post Product for Sale" use case

Following on from the first sequence diagram, Figure 9-7 shows the sequence diagram mapping onto the second use case: bid on product.

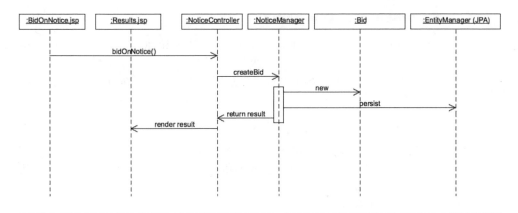

Figure 9-7   The sequence diagram for the "Bid on Product" use case

Finally, Figure 9-8 completes the three sequence diagrams necessary to provide complete coverage of the use cases detailed in Figure 9-2. In general, regardless of the level of detail or complexity that you choose to depict in your sequence diagrams, take care to ensure that the examiner can see exactly which sequence diagrams map onto the specific use cases provided.

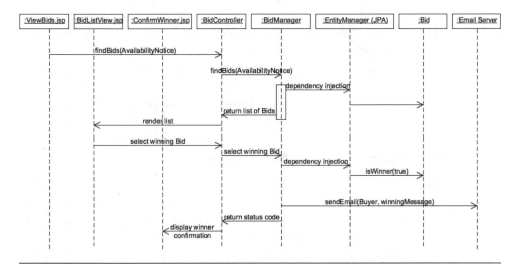

Figure 9-8   The sequence diagram for the "Select winning Bid, notify winner" use case

Comments on Diagrams

From a marking perspective, this may be the single most important sentence you will read in this entire book: *Make it easy for the examiner to find the information necessary to pass your assignment.* Specifically, do the following:

- Make all of your diagrams legible.
- Do not use tools that make "innovative" use of JavaScript to zoom in and out of—ensure that your tool outputs static images only, in line with the explicit instructions provided on acceptable file and image formats.
- From the advice given previously, you now know that the exam is all about solving a business problem using JEE—make sure that the examiner can find that business solution in your diagrams. If your class diagram is 80% frameworks and 20% business logic, it's a candidate for failure.
- By all means, augment diagrams with English text, but ensure that your diagrams hold water on their own. In an exam where UML diagrams are listed as deliverables, a clear, accurate, and easy-to-understand picture is truly worth a thousand words.

The diagrams provided in this chapter satisfy the criteria listed in the preceding bulleted list, but it is also important to remember that the diagrams provided represent only one way of documenting the information. As long as you follow the criteria listed here, feel free to provide your own unique UML diagrams that showcase your unique solution to your assigned business problem scenario.

Identified Risks and Mitigations

The new version of the exam was ostensibly re-written simply to test candidates on the JEE 5 platform. (The exam it replaced was seven years old.) However, the new exam goes further than that. Sun took the opportunity to review where the old exam format and deliverables could be improved. This section was born out of that review. In this segment of the exam, you are tested on a fundamental architect skill—the ability to recognize the top technical risks present in your allotted business scenario and to address them in your business solution.

Be strategic and objective in your assessment of risk. Many candidates in the beta lost marks by favoring low-level, avoidable risks over high-level, systemic risks that would be nightmare scenarios if they occurred. To be blunt, in an online marketplace, a security compromise in any form would be a major risk; worrying about whether or not the application could run in multiple browsers is not. (This example is taken from a beta candidate's solution.) In this section, it is reasonable to say that the major risks that candidates should identify across all potential scenarios will be remarkably similar. Their mitigation, and hopefully complete removal, will be more specific to the individual scenario.

Part III—Defending Your Architecture

In Part III of the exam, you are asked to substantiate and justify specific decisions you made in your solution design. Remember that you are not being asked to prove that your solution is bulletproof; rather you are being asked to show that you understood the business requirements, used the JEE platform in the optimal way to meet those requirements, and that it is likely that your proposed solution will meet those requirements. You are also expected to have a clear view on the alternatives you considered and why you rejected them.

You should have a clear view on the following non-functional characteristics of the application and why your solution meets and or exceeds the requirements for all:

- Performance
- Scalability
- Reliability
- Security
- Availability
- Maintainability

You should also understand and appreciate the main technical risks inherent in both the scenario and your proposed solution and prepare mitigations for each.

Essential Points

- Clarity is essential—make it easy for the examiner to quickly and concisely understand your proposed solution.
- As you develop and document your solution, ask yourself these questions to keep your solution on track:
  - Am I providing a solution to the business problem posed, or am I solving what I want to solve?
  - Is my solution clearly documented—when I read my solution, does it reflect my intent?
  - Is my solution as simple as it can be, while clearly solving the business problem as presented to me in the scenario?
- A good test is to give your UML diagrams to a friend or co-worker (without showing them the scenario) and ask them what they think you are working on. If they can explain it back to you, great; if not, it is likely that your solution, or at least how it is documented, is not good enough and needs further work and clarification on your part.
- Remember that Sun Microsystems use a bank of exam scenarios to ensure fairness across the candidate population and that old scenarios are retired and new ones are added to the bank on a regular basis. It is possible that you will receive a scenario relating to an industry vertical that you know well. In fact, you may feel the urge to provide a solution taking into account your a priori knowledge. Resist this temptation! The exam is not testing your knowledge of financial derivatives or the oil and gas transportation industry; rather, these are simplified of their real-world equivalents designed to test just one thing—can you architect a good solution to a given problem? That's all. There are no points for a solution to the real-world problem; in fact, candidates who adopt this approach tend to either fail or achieve just a low-scoring pass mark because they are not answering the questions posed in the assignment.
- Ensure that your solution is delivered in a vendor-neutral format. The exam instructions are clear on this point—your solution must be readable in any browser and must not use vendor-specific extensions or file formats. This is basic stuff, but some candidates make this error every year.

Index

A

Abstract Factory pattern, 101-102
active replication, 29
activity diagrams, 160
Adapter pattern, 107-108
adornments, 155
aggregation, 154
AJAX (Asynchronous JavaScript and XML), 46
Alexander, Christopher, 99
algorithms, load balancing, 25
Alur, Deepak, 100
annotational elements (UML), 153
annotations for web services, 61
APIs
    JAXB, 72
    JAXR, 73
Application Controller pattern, 129
application infrastructure layer, 19
Application Service pattern, 135-136
architects, characteristics of, 5-6
architecture
    creating, 4-6
    decomposition, 13-14
        availability improvements, 28-29
        dimensions, 23-24
        extensibility improvements, 29
        layers, 18-20
        performance improvements, 27-28

redundancy improvements, 24-27
        scalability improvements, 30
        service-level requirements, 20-22
        strategies, 14-17
        tiers, 17-18, 30-32
    defending, 179
    defined, 2-4, 32
    mechanisms, 3
    patterns, 99
    versus design, 4
asymmetric clusters, 27
Asynchronous JavaScript and XML (AJAX), 46
authentication, 86
authorization, 86-87
availability, 21
    defined, 33
    improvements, 28-29

B

Bean Managed Persistence (BMP) entity beans, 57
beans. See EJBs
Beck, Kent, 100
behavior diagrams
    activity diagrams, 160
    interaction diagrams, 163
behavioral elements (UML), 152-153

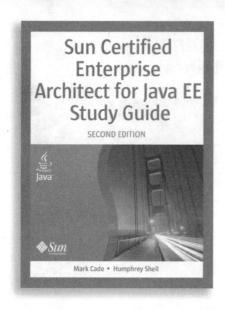

FREE Online Edition

Your purchase of **Sun Certified Enterprise Architect for Java™ EE Study Guide** includes access to a free online edition for 45 days through the Safari Books Online subscription service. Nearly every Prentice Hall book is available online through Safari Books Online, along with more than 5,000 other technical books and videos from publishers such as Addison-Wesley Professional, Cisco Press, Exam Cram, IBM Press, O'Reilly, Que, and Sams.

SAFARI BOOKS ONLINE allows you to search for a specific answer, cut and paste code, download chapters, and stay current with emerging technologies.

Activate your FREE Online Edition at
www.informit.com/safarifree

> **STEP 1:** Enter the coupon code: PSQUQGA.

> **STEP 2:** New Safari users, complete the brief registration form.
> Safari subscribers, just log in.

If you have difficulty registering on Safari or accessing the online edition,
please e-mail customer-service@safaribooksonline.com